The AI & ML Product Manager

From Zero to Offer Interview Playbook

LUIS JURADO

INDEX

Objectives of the Book 9

How to Use This Book 15

Part I: Foundation of AI/ML Product Management 21

    Chapter 1: Understanding AI/ML 25

    Chapter 2: Role of a Product Manager in AI/ML 35

    Chapter 3: Essential Skills for AI/ML Product Managers 53

Part II: Preparing for Your AI/ML PM Interview 94

    Chapter 4: Understanding the AI/ML PM Job Market 98

    Chapter 5: Crafting an Impactful AI/ML PM Resume 107

    Chapter 6: Writing a Convincing Cover Letter 116

    Chapter 7: Conducting In-depth Company Research 137

Part III: The AI/ML PM Interview Process 144

    The AI/ML PM Interview Process 144

    Chapter 10: The Screening Interview 166

    Chapter 11: The Technical Interview 177

    Chapter 12: The Behavioral Interview 195

Part IV: Interviewing Mastery 216

    Chapter 13: The Case Study Interview 221

    Chapter 14: The On-site Interview 230

    Chapter 15: Negotiating Your Offer 242

    Chapter 16: Common AI/ML PM Interview Questions 254

    Chapter 17: Post-Interview Tips 285

Part V: Succeeding and Advancing in Your AI/ML Product Manager Career **299**

Chapter 19: Building Relationships and Influence 306

Chapter 20: Staying Up to Date in AI/ML 312

Chapter 21: Career Advancement for AI/ML PMs 316

Chapter 22: Continuous Learning and Growth 322

Reflections **326**

Next Steps **329**

NOTES **332**

BIBLIOGRAPHY **336**

About the author **338**

WELCOME

Welcome, to From Zero to Offer: The AI & ML Product Manager's Interview Playbook. Whether you're a newcomer entering the technology sector, an established professional looking to pivot into a more dynamic and future-focused area, or an ambitious student eager to jumpstart a career in product management, this book has been written expressly for you.

It's a common understanding that the worlds of artificial intelligence (AI) and machine learning (ML) are growing at an exponential pace. They are not only driving changes in our daily lives, from our smartphones to our household appliances, but also transforming industries, from healthcare to finance, manufacturing, and beyond. These areas are teeming with opportunities, particularly in product management roles, where you have the chance to bridge the gap between complex technologies and their practical applications.

But while the opportunities are abundant, so too are the challenges. Securing a role in AI/ML product management is no small feat. It requires a comprehensive understanding of these sophisticated technologies, a robust set of soft and hard skills, and the ability to navigate the often intricate maze of job hunting and interviewing. Furthermore, once you've landed a role, the journey only just begins as you strive to make an impact, continue learning, and advance your career.

From Zero to Offer aims to be your faithful companion throughout this journey. This playbook takes you through the world of AI/ML product management, from understanding the fundamentals of these technologies to mastering the art of the job interview and succeeding in your role.

However, this is not a book that you'll read once and then consign to the back of a shelf. Instead, consider it a trusted resource to refer back to time and again as you progress through your career. We've aimed to make each section standalone, allowing you to easily flip to the chapters most relevant to you at any given time.

In Part I, we lay down the foundational knowledge required for any AI/ML product manager. Here, we demystify the complex jargon and introduce the key principles of AI and ML, and dive deep into the unique role that a product manager plays in this sphere.

Part II, on the other hand, is all about the preparation for the AI/ML product manager interview. We will guide you on understanding the job market, crafting an impactful resume, writing a convincing cover letter, and conducting in-depth company research. This section also discusses networking strategies and deciphers the often-cryptic job descriptions.

Part III delves into the various stages of the AI/ML PM interview process, from the initial screening to the on-site interview, including the various types of interviews you might encounter such as technical, behavioural, and case study. It also addresses a crucial yet often overlooked stage of the process: negotiating your offer.

In Part IV, we aim to equip you with the strategies and tactics for mastering the interview process. We present common interview questions and provide you with methodologies for answering them confidently. This section also provides tips for the crucial post-interview phase.

Finally, in Part V, we look at what happens once you've secured the job. The first 90 days in a new role can be challenging, but we provide a roadmap to help you navigate this period successfully. This part also discusses building relationships, staying up-to-date in AI/ML, and strategies for advancing your career in this fast-paced and constantly evolving field.

In essence, "From Zero to Offer" is designed to be both a guide and a companion, not only helping you understand the world of AI/ML product management but also providing practical, actionable advice for landing a job and succeeding in your role.

This book is the result of countless interviews with successful AI/ML product managers, recruiters, hiring managers, and leaders in the field. We've synthesised their insights and experiences into a comprehensive guide that covers every stage of your journey, from understanding the fundamental concepts of AI and ML to landing a job and making your mark in your new role.

As you delve into the pages of this playbook, I invite you to approach the content with an open and inquisitive mind. Ask questions, challenge assumptions, and most importantly, take the insights that resonate with you and apply them in your own journey. Remember, there is no one-size-fits-all approach to becoming an AI/ML product manager. Each journey is unique and filled with its own challenges and triumphs.

The fields of AI and ML are characterised by rapid change and continuous evolution. But remember, amidst the barrage of new algorithms, technologies, and terminologies, the core of product management remains the same: creating products that solve problems, deliver value, and make a meaningful impact on users' lives.

It is my sincere hope that this book will prove a valuable resource as you navigate the exciting landscape of AI and ML product management. It is a field that demands continuous learning, adaptability, and a keen sense of curiosity. But for those who are up for the challenge, it offers unparalleled opportunities to shape the future of technology and society.

Welcome to your journey from zero to offer. The path may be challenging, but with determination, passion, and the insights from this book, you are well-equipped to navigate your way to success.

Thank you for choosing "From Zero to Offer: The AI & ML Product Manager's Interview Playbook." Here's to your success in the exhilarating world of AI and ML product management.

Objectives of the Book

In the fast-paced and constantly evolving landscape of technology, breaking through and making a substantial impact can often appear to be an overwhelmingly complex challenge. This is especially true in the innovative realms of artificial intelligence (AI) and machine learning (ML). However, these are not insurmountable challenges but rather opportunities ripe for the taking. And it is precisely with this mindset that this playbook, "From Zero to Offer: The AI & ML Product Manager's Interview Playbook," has been crafted and developed.

Navigating the path to becoming an AI/ML product manager requires more than just an understanding of technology. It necessitates a holistic approach that encompasses the breadth of skills required, the market dynamics, and the myriad considerations unique to the AI and ML landscape. This comprehensive approach forms the core of our book's objective: to equip you with the knowledge, strategies, and skills necessary to not only step into but also thrive in the role of an AI/ML product manager.

AI and ML stand at the forefront of technological innovation. They are dramatically reshaping our world, fueling advancements in virtually every industry, from healthcare to finance, retail to manufacturing, and far beyond. As such, these areas represent fields of immense potential and opportunity. However, the flip side of this vast potential is the complexity and often intimidating nature of these technologies.

This book has been crafted with several core objectives in mind.

1. Demystifying AI and ML

For the uninitiated, AI and ML can appear quite intimidating. However, behind the jargon and complex algorithms, these are technologies that are truly transformative and empowering. One of the primary objectives of this book is to demystify AI and ML, breaking down these complex concepts into comprehensible components. We want to help you understand these technologies, not just from a theoretical perspective but also in terms of their practical applications and the possibilities they unlock.

2. Understand the Role of AI/ML Product Manager

A critical part of this book's mission is to provide a comprehensive understanding of the role of an AI/ML product manager. This position is a nexus between multiple disciplines, requiring a unique blend of skills and understanding. It is our objective to delineate what it means to be a product manager in the AI/ML landscape, what the job entails, and the unique challenges and rewards it presents.

3. Guide Through the AI/ML PM Job Market

The AI/ML PM job market is dynamic and competitive. To thrive, you need to understand how this market operates and how to position yourself strategically within it. This book aims to guide you through the intricacies of the job market, from identifying promising opportunities to understanding the requirements of different roles and companies.

4. Navigating the Interview Process
One of the most daunting stages in the pursuit of any job is the interview process. It can be especially challenging for AI/ML PM roles, which may require demonstrating a diverse range of skills and competencies. Our objective is to equip you with strategies and insights to confidently navigate every stage of the interview process, from initial screening to technical and behavioural interviews and all the way through to the final on-site interview.

5. Preparing for Career Success
Securing the job is just the first step in your journey as an AI/ML product manager. This book also aims to prepare you for long-term career success. From making the most of your first 90 days to building relationships and staying up-to-date with industry trends and strategies for career advancement – we seek to provide a comprehensive guide to succeeding and excelling in your role.

6. A Tool for Continuous Learning
AI and ML are fields characterised by continuous change and evolution. The learning, therefore, never stops. This book is designed to be a tool for continuous learning, a resource that you can return to time and again throughout your career. Whether you're preparing for an interview, tackling a new challenge at work, or considering the next

step in your career, we aim to provide relevant and useful insights.

7. Empower Through Real-World Insights

This book is enriched by real-world insights from successful AI/ML product managers, recruiters, hiring managers, and industry leaders. By sharing their experiences, wisdom, and advice, we aim to give you a nuanced and practical understanding of what it takes to succeed as an AI/ML product manager.

8. Inclusive and Accessible

Lastly, we believe that everyone, regardless of their background or prior experience, should have the opportunity to pursue a career in AI/ML product management. One of our key objectives is to make this field accessible to all. We've strived to write this book in a way that is inclusive, straightforward, and jargon-free as much as possible. Whether you're a recent graduate, a seasoned professional looking to pivot, or even someone with no prior experience in technology, this book is designed to be a helpful resource.

9. Foster a Community of Learners

The journey to becoming an AI/ML product manager is not one that should be undertaken alone. It is our objective to foster a community of learners, providing a platform for readers to engage, exchange ideas, and support one another. By reading this book, you become part of a broader community of individuals passionate about AI/ML and keen on building a career in this domain.

10. Encourage Ethical Practice

In the fast-paced world of AI and ML, ethical considerations often take a backseat. However, as product managers in this sphere, we must remember that the decisions we make can have profound societal implications. Thus, one of our key objectives is to encourage ethical practice, ensuring that readers understand the importance of fairness, transparency, and accountability in AI/ML.

11. Provide a Comprehensive Resource

Finally, our objective is to provide a comprehensive resource for all things related to AI/ML product management. From understanding the fundamentals of AI/ML, and preparing for interviews to navigating the intricacies of the job, this book aims to be a one-stop-shop that equips you with the knowledge, tools, and confidence needed to launch and advance your career.

In essence, "From Zero to Offer: The AI and ML Product Manager's Interview Playbook" seeks to bridge the gap between ambition and reality. It is our sincere hope that the insights, strategies, and advice contained within these pages empower you to traverse the exciting, challenging, and immensely rewarding journey to becoming an AI/ML product manager.

As you turn the pages of this playbook, remember that every journey is unique, and the ultimate measure of success is the growth you experience along the way. Embark on this journey with an open mind, a willingness to learn, and a relentless drive to make a meaningful impact in the field of AI and ML.

We are thrilled to accompany you on this journey and look forward to the amazing things you will accomplish. Here's to your journey from zero to offer and beyond.

How to Use This Book

Thank you for embarking on this journey with us through "From Zero to Offer: The AI & ML Product Manager's Interview Playbook". To maximise the value and impact of this playbook, we would like to provide guidance on navigating and using this book effectively.

1. Start from the Beginning

Although it might be tempting to skip ahead to the sections that seem immediately relevant, we strongly recommend starting from the beginning. This book has been carefully structured to build your knowledge and skills progressively. The foundational concepts of AI and ML presented in the initial chapters provide a basis upon which later chapters expand. The strategies and advice in the later sections will be more meaningful and valuable with a solid understanding of these foundational elements.

2. Active Reading

While reading, try to engage actively with the material. This involves thinking critically about what you are reading, asking questions, and drawing connections to your own experiences and knowledge. Instead of passively absorbing information, reflect on the implications of what you are reading. How does it relate to what you already know? How can you apply it in your situation? This approach not only enhances comprehension but also facilitates the application of knowledge.

3. Use the Workbook and Tools

Throughout the book, you will find various tools and exercises designed to aid your understanding and application of the material. This includes self-assessment quizzes, reflection questions, practical exercises, and real-world case studies. Make full use of these tools. They provide an opportunity to put what you're learning into practice and to assess your progress.

4. Take Notes

Note-taking is a powerful tool for enhancing comprehension and retention. When you come across a particularly insightful passage, a piece of advice you find useful, or a concept you find challenging, jot it down. Over time, these notes can serve as a quick reference guide, a tool for revision, and a means of tracking your learning journey.

5. Revisit and Review

Learning is rarely a linear process. You might not understand a concept completely the first time around, or you might find that an idea or strategy becomes more relevant or meaningful over time. Don't hesitate to revisit earlier chapters or sections. Regular review not only reinforces what you've learned but can also provide fresh insights.

6. Engage with the Community

Remember, you are not alone on this journey. By reading this book, you become part of a community of aspiring AI/ML product managers. Engage with this community. Share your insights, ask questions, learn from the experiences of others, and provide support to your peers. The exchange of ideas and perspectives can significantly enrich your learning experience.

7. Apply What You Learn
This book is not just about acquiring knowledge; it's about applying that knowledge. As you progress through the chapters, think about how you can put what you're learning into practice. This could involve tailoring your resume, practising interview responses, or applying the concepts of AI/ML to a project or problem in your current role.

8. Remember, It's a Marathon, Not a Sprint
Becoming an AI/ML product manager is a journey, not a destination. It requires continuous learning and development. Don't rush through the book in a bid to hasten this process. Take your time. Reflect on what you're learning. Experiment with different strategies. Learn from mistakes. Enjoy the process of learning and growth.

9. Be Open-Minded
The field of AI and ML is vast and diverse. There is no one 'right' way to be a product manager in this field. Different roles, companies, and industries may require different approaches, skillsets, and strategies. Be open to exploring different paths and perspectives. Embrace diversity and complexity. Stay flexible and adaptable in your learning journey.

10. Build on the book
This book is a comprehensive guide, but it's not the be-all and end-all of AI/ML product management. It's a stepping

stone, a solid foundation upon which you can build. Use this book as a launchpad for further learning. Seek out additional resources, keep up with the latest developments in AI and ML, and continue to develop your skills and knowledge even after you've finished reading.

11. Practice Self-Care

Embarking on a new career or a new role can be exciting but also challenging and, at times, stressful. Remember to take care of yourself throughout this process. Make sure to balance your dedication to learning and development with ample time for relaxation and leisure. Don't hesitate to seek support if you're feeling overwhelmed or unsure. Your well-being is as crucial to your success as your technical skills and knowledge.

12. Embrace Uncertainty

Uncertainty is a given in any learning journey, especially in a dynamic and rapidly evolving field such as AI and ML. You might encounter concepts that need to be clarified or face challenges that seem insurmountable. But remember, Uncertainty is a part of the process. It's a sign that you're stepping out of your comfort zone, challenging your assumptions, and expanding your horizons. Embrace Uncertainty. Persevere through difficulties. Celebrate your progress, however small it may seem.

13. Use the Resources and References

At the end of this book, you'll find a set of resources and references. These include further readings, websites, online courses, and communities that can enhance your understanding and skills in AI and ML. They can also provide more nuanced and diverse perspectives, augmenting the material presented in this book. We recommend exploring these resources to deepen your learning and connect with the broader AI and ML community.

14. Feedback is Welcome

Finally, remember that this book is for you. We value your feedback, insights, and experiences. Whether you have a suggestion for improving the book, a question about a specific topic, or a real-life experience you'd like to share, we welcome your input. By sharing your feedback, you not only contribute to your own learning journey but also to those of future readers.

In conclusion, this book has been designed to be more than just a passive source of information. It is an interactive, comprehensive guide to help you navigate your journey towards becoming an AI/ML product manager. Whether you're a newcomer to the field or a seasoned professional seeking to update your skills, "From Zero to Offer: The AI & ML Product Manager's Interview Playbook" is here to support you every step of the way.

Remember, the ultimate aim of this book is not to provide you with all the answers but to equip you with the tools, strategies, and mindset you need to find your own path and make your own mark in the field of AI and ML product management. Your journey starts here, and we look forward to accompanying you as you turn your ambition into reality.

Good luck, and here's to your journey from zero to offer and beyond.

Part I

Foundation of

AI/ML Product Management

The AI and ML product management space, is fascinating and invigorating, teeming with potential, fraught with challenges, and brimming with opportunities. As you embark on this journey, it's vital to grasp the foundational elements of AI/ML product management. This part of the book, divided into three chapters, serves to provide you with that groundwork.

Before we delve deeper into the subject, let's define what an AI/ML product manager is. An AI/ML product manager, at their core, is a bridge. They connect the highly technical aspects of AI and ML to the practical aspects of product development. They communicate the capabilities and limitations of AI/ML technology to stakeholders, translate business requirements into technical goals, and ensure that AI/ML deployments are aligned with user needs and business objectives.

Now that we've established what an AI/ML product manager does let's explore the foundational elements of AI/ML product management.

Understanding AI and ML
The first foundational block in this journey is a solid understanding of AI and ML, as we outlined in the first chapter. As a product manager, you're not required to master the technical intricacies of these technologies, but you should understand their capabilities, limitations, and use cases. You should be able to comprehend how these technologies work, how they can add value, and how they can be integrated into products.

Role of a Product Manager in AI/ML

The second foundational block is an understanding of the role of a product manager in an AI/ML context. AI/ML product management is distinct from conventional product management. AI/ML product managers must grapple with unique challenges, such as the unpredictable nature of ML models, the importance of data quality, and the ethical implications of AI.

At the same time, they must fulfil the traditional responsibilities of product managers, such as defining the product vision, communicating with stakeholders, and overseeing the product lifecycle. In essence, an AI/ML product manager is a hybrid role that requires a blend of technical expertise, strategic thinking, and leadership skills.

Essential Skills for AI/ML Product Managers

The third foundational block is the development of essential skills for AI/ML product management. AI/ML product managers need a unique set of skills that combine the technical, the strategic, and the interpersonal.
On the technical side, they need to understand AI/ML algorithms, data infrastructure, and software development processes. On the strategic side, they need to master product strategy, user experience design, and data-driven decision-making. On the interpersonal side, they need to excel at communication, collaboration, and leadership.

Each of these foundational elements is critical to becoming a successful AI/ML product manager. They provide the knowledge, perspective, and skills you need to navigate the complex and dynamic landscape of AI/ML product management. But remember, mastering these elements is not an end in itself. It's the beginning of a journey, a launching pad for your growth and evolution as an AI/ML product manager.

As we move through this part of the book, we'll explore each of these foundational elements in depth. We'll delve into the complexities of AI and ML, dissect the role of an AI/ML product manager, and unpack the essential skills for AI/ML product management. We'll provide practical insights, real-world examples, and actionable strategies to help you build a solid foundation in AI/ML product management.

Part I is about setting the stage for your journey. It's about preparing you to navigate the challenging, exhilarating world of AI/ML product management. As you delve into these chapters, remember to keep an open mind, stay curious, and embrace the learning process.

Remember, the foundation you build today will shape the AI/ML product manager you become tomorrow. So let's dive in, explore, and lay the groundwork for your success. Welcome to the fascinating world of AI/ML product management.

Chapter 1

Understanding AI/ML

At the dawn of the 21st century, the world stands on the brink of a technological revolution. This revolution, unlike any preceding it, is being fuelled by the twin forces of artificial intelligence (AI) and machine learning (ML). From autonomous vehicles to personalised recommendation systems, AI and ML are not just transforming how we work, live, and communicate but are also reshaping the very fabric of our society and economy.

This chapter aims to provide a foundational understanding of these two critical and intertwined fields. By the end of this chapter, you should have a solid grasp of what AI and ML are, why they matter, and how they're used in the context of product management.

Artificial Intelligence: The New Electricity

Often compared to electricity for its potential to transform industries and lives, artificial intelligence (AI) is a branch of computer science concerned with creating systems capable of performing tasks that usually require human intelligence. These tasks encompass a wide range of activities, including recognising speech, understanding natural language, identifying images, and making decisions.

AI is often seen as a futuristic concept, but it is already embedded in our everyday lives. If you've ever asked Siri a question, received recommendations from Netflix, or used Google Maps to navigate, you've interacted with AI. AI's growing presence across industries and applications underscores its transformative power and potential.

AI systems can be broadly categorised into two types: narrow AI and general AI. Narrow AI, also known as weak AI, is designed to perform specific tasks, such as voice recognition or image analysis. Most of the AI we interact with today falls into this category.

General AI, or strong AI, on the other hand, refers to systems capable of understanding, learning, and applying knowledge across a broad range of tasks, much like a human. While general AI is a fascinating concept, it remains largely within the realm of science fiction. Our focus in this book is on narrow AI, given its immediate relevance and impact on product management.

Machine Learning: AI's Driving Force

Machine learning (ML) is a subfield of AI that's crucial to making AI systems work. In essence, ML is a method of data analysis that automates the building of analytical models. It empowers computers to learn from data, identify patterns, and make decisions with minimal human intervention.

ML models learn from experience. The more data they're exposed to, the better they get at predicting and making informed decisions. For instance, an ML model can be trained to recognise spam emails by analysing thousands of examples. Over time, the model learns the characteristics that distinguish spam emails and can accurately classify new emails.

ML is behind many of the most exciting and innovative applications of AI. It powers Google's search engine, Facebook's automatic tagging feature, and Amazon's recommendation system. In the realm of product management, ML algorithms are used to analyse user behaviour, personalise user experiences, and predict future trends.

There are three main types of machine learning: supervised learning, unsupervised learning, and reinforcement learning.

- Supervised learning involves training an ML model on a labelled dataset, i.e., a dataset where the desired output is known. This type of learning is commonly used for tasks such as spam detection and image recognition.

- Unsupervised learning, in contrast, involves training an ML model on an unlabelled dataset. The model is left to identify patterns and relationships in the data on its own. This type of learning is often used for tasks such as customer segmentation and anomaly detection.
- Reinforcement learning involves an agent learning to make decisions by interacting with an environment. The agent receives rewards or penalties based on its actions, which it uses to learn and improve its decision-making over time. This type of learning is commonly used in applications like game-playing AI, robotics, and self-driving cars.

The Importance of AI and ML

As we move through the 21st century, the significance of AI and ML in the realm of business has become evident. These advanced technologies once considered the domain of science fiction, are now firmly in the realm of business realities. They are transforming industries and redefining the way we conduct business. This transformation is so pervasive that understanding AI and ML is now a crucial requirement for professionals in a range of roles, including product managers.

Product managers need to understand AI, and ML stems from their potential to change the essence of products and services. These technologies offer businesses the opportunity to explore new territories, delivering an edge in the intensely competitive world of product management.

The first significant advantage AI and ML confer is their ability to generate insights. By leveraging AI and ML, product managers can dig into vast amounts of data, mining it for valuable insights that might otherwise remain hidden. These insights can reveal patterns and trends, identify user preferences and habits, and even predict future behaviours. The result is a wealth of knowledge that can drive product strategy, influence design choices, and shape the positioning of products in the marketplace. In short, AI and ML can help product managers make more informed, data-driven decisions.

Next, AI and ML can be used to enhance the functionality of products and enrich the user experience. By integrating AI and ML capabilities into products, product managers can create features that are not just intelligent but also personalised and engaging. Think about features like voice recognition, real-time recommendations, or personalisation algorithms. These features can elevate a product from being merely useful to being extraordinary, increasing the product's value and users' satisfaction.

In addition, understanding AI and ML can improve collaboration between product managers and technical teams. A sound understanding of these technologies enables product managers to fully grasp what's technically feasible and what's not. It allows them to communicate more effectively with engineers and data scientists, bridging the gap between the technical and non-technical domains. Moreover, it enables them to make informed decisions about technology trade-offs, balancing the potential of AI and ML against factors like cost, time, and resource constraints.

The implications of AI and ML extend even beyond these areas. They affect how businesses interact with customers, how they manage their operations, and even how they strategise for the future. AI and ML have become essential tools for businesses looking to stay ahead of the curve in a rapidly evolving digital landscape.

However, the journey towards integrating AI and ML into product management isn't without its challenges. It requires a shift in mindset, a willingness to learn, and an ability to adapt. It's a journey that demands a balance of technical understanding, strategic thinking, and leadership. Yet, for those who undertake this journey, the rewards can be immense.

AI and ML: The Future of Product Management

As we commence this book, the first point of discussion is a clear understanding of the role Artificial Intelligence (AI), and Machine Learning (ML) are set to play in the future of product management. These innovative technologies are not simply trends or passing fads but powerful forces destined to revolutionise product management entirely.

The world is witnessing an unprecedented evolution in the field of technology, with AI and ML taking centre stage. AI refers to systems or machines that mimic human intelligence to perform tasks and make decisions, while ML, a subset of AI, refers to systems that can learn from and make decisions based on data.

The potency of AI and ML lies in their transformative potential. AI and ML technologies can analyse vast quantities of data more quickly and accurately than humans. They can identify patterns, predict trends, automate tasks, personalise experiences, and even make decisions. In the product management sphere, this opens up a wealth of opportunities.

AI and ML are not just enhancing existing products; they're facilitating the creation of entirely new ones. From self-driving cars to personalised recommendation engines, these technologies are redefining what products can do.

Consequently, they're also redefining what it means to be a product manager.

Today's product managers need to understand how to translate the capabilities of AI and ML into practical, user-centric product features. They need to manage the AI/ML product lifecycle, from ideation through to launch and iteration. They also need to navigate the complex ethical and societal implications of these technologies, ensuring that products are not just intelligent but also responsible.

Moreover, the advent of AI and ML is shifting user expectations. Users are becoming accustomed to personalised, predictive, and seamless experiences – expectations that are challenging to meet without the use of AI and ML. As a result, these technologies are becoming less of an optional extra and more of a necessary ingredient in the product management mix.

Yet, the introduction of AI and ML also amplifies market competition. Companies that harness these technologies effectively can create superior products, gain a competitive edge, and even disrupt entire industries. For product managers, understanding AI and ML is not just about staying relevant; it's about staying ahead.

But the journey of understanding AI and ML goes beyond surface-level comprehension. It calls for a robust, nuanced, and critical understanding that can be applied across different contexts and roles. It requires a balance of technical knowledge, strategic insight, ethical considerations, and leadership skills. And that's precisely what this book aims to deliver.

In the following chapters, we'll delve deeper into the world of AI and ML in product management. We'll explore how to effectively harness these technologies, navigate their challenges, and shape products that are not just technologically advanced but also meaningful and valuable to users.

To conclude, AI and ML are more than just technologies; they're transformative forces, reshaping the very fabric of product management. As we look towards the future, it's evident that the product managers who understand and harness these forces will be the ones who shape the future. So, as we embark on this journey of exploration and learning, we invite you to join us. After all, the future of AI and ML product management is not just something to be observed; it's something to be actively shaped.

Chapter 2

Role of a Product Manager in AI/ML

The rise of Artificial Intelligence (AI) and Machine Learning (ML) has irrevocably transformed the landscape of technology and, by extension, the role of the product manager. As the ambassadors of AI and ML in the world of product management, AI/ML Product Managers find themselves navigating uncharted waters, translating complex technical concepts into tangible product features that provide value to end-users.

No longer confined to the traditional management role, these product managers have become the conduit between the technological and business realms, tasked with bridging the gap between cutting-edge technology and practical product development. In this new world order, the AI/ML product manager is expected to be an interpreter of complex technologies, a visionary capable of predicting future trends, and an ambassador for the user experience.

These expectations significantly expand the remit of a product manager. While the fundamental principles of product management – such as strategy formulation, road mapping, cross-functional team coordination and user-centric design – remain relevant, the addition of AI and ML introduces new dimensions to these responsibilities.

An AI/ML product manager needs to have a firm grasp of these technologies and understand their potential, limitations, and applications. They need to understand the language of data scientists and engineers, translating it into the language of business benefits and user needs. They need to be able to see the big picture, anticipating how AI and ML will shape the future of their industry and adjusting their product strategies accordingly.

Yet, their role doesn't stop at understanding and strategising. They must also be able to articulate the value of AI and ML to stakeholders, from executives to customers. They need to champion these technologies, addressing misconceptions, allaying fears, and demonstrating the tangible benefits that AI and ML can deliver. This requires not only a technical understanding of AI and ML but also strong communication and leadership skills.

Moreover, in the rapidly evolving field of AI and ML, product managers must be agile learners. The pace of technological change requires them to continuously update their knowledge and skills, staying abreast of the latest developments, methodologies, and tools. They must be comfortable with ambiguity and uncertainty, making decisions based on incomplete or rapidly changing information.

At the same time, they must navigate the ethical implications of AI and ML, advocating for the responsible use of these technologies. They need to be mindful of the societal impact of their products, considering issues such as data privacy, algorithmic bias, and job displacement.

Finally, the AI/ML product manager must not lose sight of the ultimate goal – to create products that deliver value to users. Amid all the complexities and challenges of AI and ML, they need to remain steadfast in their commitment to the user, ensuring that technology serves as a tool to enhance, rather than complicate, the user experience.

As we venture further into this chapter, we will delve deeper into each of these aspects of the AI/ML product manager's role, providing practical insights and guidance to help you navigate this complex yet exhilarating terrain. The journey may be challenging, but it promises to be a rewarding one, offering a glimpse into the future of product management – a future where AI and ML are not just tools but strategic drivers of product success.

The Product Manager: A Brief Refresher

Being a product manager involves a comprehensive, 360-degree perspective on the product. It calls for overseeing the product's journey from ideation to market launch and beyond, requiring a diverse skill set that spans across multiple domains. At the heart of this role lies a strategic vision, a deep understanding of user needs, and a keen sense of market dynamics.

The product manager, in essence, is the person who stands at the intersection of business, technology, and user experience. They are visionaries who define the product strategy, mapping out a product roadmap that aligns with the company's strategic objectives, market trends, and customer needs. They are responsible for conceptualising the product, validating its feasibility, and establishing its value proposition. This strategic dimension necessitates a blend of analytical acumen, market insight, and strategic foresight.

On the development front, the product manager acts as the pivotal link between the engineering team and other stakeholders. They collaborate closely with the engineering team, translating business requirements into technical specifications, prioritising features, and managing the product backlog. They ensure that development efforts align with the product vision and that the final product delivers on its promised value. This facet of their role demands technical proficiency, project management skills, and an ability to foster cross-functional collaboration.

In terms of marketing and communication, the product manager is tasked with conveying the product's value to the external world, encompassing customers, stakeholders, and the market at large. They work hand in hand with marketing teams to design go-to-market strategies, craft compelling product narratives, and manage product launches. Moreover, they communicate internally with stakeholders, managing expectations and ensuring alignment across the board. This aspect of their role calls for exceptional communication skills, creativity, and an understanding of marketing principles.

The product manager is also a custodian of user needs and interests. They employ various tools and techniques to capture user feedback, understand user behaviours, and uncover user needs. This information is then used to refine the product, enhance user experience, and drive product decisions. In doing so, they place the user at the heart of product development, ensuring that the product not only solves user problems but also delights them in the process. This user-centric dimension of their role requires empathy, user research skills, and a commitment to continuous improvement.

In the context of AI/ML, these core responsibilities remain steadfast. However, the way these responsibilities are carried out is augmented by the unique capabilities of AI and ML technologies. As we move forward, we'll delve into how the role of the product manager is transformed when we introduce the power of AI and ML into the mix. We'll explore how these technologies can be harnessed to generate insights, enhance product capabilities, and create a product that not only meets user needs but also pushes the boundaries of what is possible.

The AI/ML Product Manager: Adding a New Layer

With the advent of AI and ML, product management has not only evolved but metamorphosed, adding a layer of complexity that demands a unique set of skills and competencies. While the foundational responsibilities remain, the arena of AI/ML adds a new dimension that enriches the role of the product manager, augmenting it with a novel blend of challenges and opportunities.

At its core, product management revolves around creating products that solve user problems, add value, and are commercially viable. This fundamental principle does not change with AI/ML. However, what does change is the way in which this is accomplished. AI/ML introduces a fresh perspective on problem-solving, offering a new set of tools that can be harnessed to enhance product capabilities and user experiences. Consequently, the role of the product manager in this context becomes multifaceted.

Product managers working with AI and ML are not only responsible for guiding product development but are also tasked with envisioning how these emerging technologies can be leveraged to create innovative solutions. This requires an understanding of AI and ML algorithms and methodologies, the ability to collaborate effectively with data scientists and engineers, and the foresight to anticipate how these technologies can be utilised to solve user problems and tap into new market opportunities.

Moreover, AI/ML product managers are entrusted with the task of demystifying these complex technologies to stakeholders. From translating the intricacies of machine learning models to non-technical teams to articulating the benefits of AI-powered features to users and stakeholders – communication forms a crucial part of their role. This new layer, therefore, necessitates a blend of technical proficiency, strategic thinking, and exceptional communication skills.

This added layer also brings with it a new set of ethical considerations. AI/ML technologies, while powerful, can pose risks related to privacy, bias, and security. Hence, an AI/ML product manager must navigate these ethical waters, ensuring responsible use of technology and addressing these concerns proactively.

Finally, with the incorporation of AI and ML, product management becomes a more iterative and data-driven process. AI/ML product managers are required to establish robust feedback loops, continuously gather and analyse data, and refine their products based on this analysis. This requirement adds a degree of analytical rigour to the role, necessitating comfort with data and metrics.

To encapsulate, AI and ML add a significant layer to the role of product management. They extend the product manager's remit, pushing them to become experts not only in their product but also in transformative technology.

However, this added layer is not an unwieldy burden; it's an exciting progression that provides product managers with a rich palette of tools to craft solutions that were previously unimaginable.

Technical Liaison

Building on their role as an intermediary between various stakeholders, an AI/ML product manager shoulders a unique responsibility in the field of AI/ML product development. This responsibility emerges from the complex nature of AI/ML technologies, which often presents a steep learning curve for non-technical stakeholders. It is the product manager's task to bridge this gap, demystifying AI/ML and facilitating a clear understanding of its capabilities and limitations.

This requires an ability to communicate complex technical concepts in a simple, accessible language. The product manager should be able to explain what AI/ML can do and what it can't, what it requires to function effectively (such as data, algorithms, computational resources), and what kind of results it can deliver. They should be able to articulate these aspects in a way that resonates with the non-technical audience, highlighting the benefits of AI/ML without getting lost in technical jargon.

On the other hand, the AI/ML product manager also acts as the voice of the business within the technical team. They ensure that the AI/ML engineers understand the business requirements, market needs, and user expectations that the product should meet. This involves translating high-level business objectives into specific technical requirements that can guide the AI/ML development process. This, in turn, requires a solid understanding of AI/ML principles, an ability to think from a user's perspective, and effective communication skills to articulate these requirements to the technical team.

Moreover, the AI/ML product manager must manage stakeholders' expectations on both sides. For the non-technical stakeholders, this might involve setting realistic expectations about what AI/ML can achieve, how long it will take, and what resources it will require. For the technical team, this could involve aligning their work with the broader business strategy, prioritising tasks based on business value, and ensuring they have the resources to deliver the expected results.

Ultimately, the AI/ML product manager serves as a bridge that connects two very different worlds the intricate world of AI/ML technology and the pragmatic world of business needs and user expectations. It is their responsibility to ensure that these two worlds not only understand each other but also work together harmoniously towards a shared goal developing a product that harnesses the power of AI/ML to deliver significant value to users and the business.

Visionary Strategist

The arena of AI/ML offers an expansive horizon of possibilities for product development. As technologies evolve, the breadth of these possibilities is widening further. In such a dynamic landscape, the role of an AI/ML product manager extends far beyond mere translation and coordination. They act as visionary strategists who can discern valuable opportunities amidst the realm of possibilities that AI/ML presents.

As a visionary strategist, the AI/ML product manager's responsibility begins with identifying where AI/ML can create a competitive advantage. This entails a deep understanding of the product's market, including competitors, user needs and behaviours, and emerging trends. With this understanding, the product manager can spot areas where AI/ML can elevate the product's offering, whether it's through personalised user experiences, predictive capabilities, automation, or any other AI/ML-driven functionality.

Innovating user experiences is another crucial aspect of an AI/ML product manager's strategy. AI/ML technologies can be leveraged to tailor user experiences based on individual user data, driving user engagement and satisfaction. A product manager must envision these enhancements and articulate how AI/ML can manifest them.

Moreover, an AI/ML product manager can spot opportunities to improve operational efficiency using AI/ML. From streamlining processes to making data-driven decisions, AI/ML can bring substantial efficiency improvements that can reduce costs and accelerate growth. The product manager's strategic acumen plays a vital role in recognising and capitalising on these opportunities.

Upon identifying these opportunities, the AI/ML product manager must shape a compelling vision for the product that integrates these AI/ML innovations. Crafting this vision requires a deep understanding of AI/ML capabilities, a strong sense of the product's purpose, and a keen awareness of the company's broader strategy and goals.

This vision will serve as the north star guiding the product's development. It should articulate how AI/ML can enhance the product's value proposition, detailing the specific improvements in functionality, user experience, or operational efficiency that AI/ML will deliver. It should also align seamlessly with the company's wider objectives, ensuring that the AI/ML innovations contribute positively to the company's growth and success.

Guardian of Ethics

The technological prowess of AI/ML does not exist in isolation. It comes bundled with a set of ethical considerations that need to be adroitly managed. THEREFORE, the AI/ML product manager stands as the guardian of ethics, responsible for integrating these ethical considerations into every stage of product development.

Bias in data forms the first significant ethical challenge. AI/ML algorithms are only as good as the data that trains them. If this data is tainted with bias, it will reflect in the predictions or recommendations that the AI/ML models make. For instance, if a product's AI/ML algorithm is trained on data that represents a narrow demographic segment, it might not perform well or even act discriminatorily against users outside that segment. As a product manager, it falls upon you to ensure that the data is representative of the diverse user base and free from undue biases.

The second ethical challenge revolves around privacy. AI/ML products often rely on collecting and processing vast amounts of user data. As a product manager, it is your responsibility to ensure that this data collection aligns with privacy regulations and respects user privacy. You must be transparent about what data is collected, how it is used, and provide users with control over their data.

Transparency in decision-making constitutes the third ethical issue. AI/ML algorithms, particularly deep learning models, are often criticised for being "black boxes", making decisions without providing clear explanations. As a product manager, you should strive to make the product's AI/ML-driven decisions as transparent and explainable as possible. This can involve working with your technical team to implement explainable AI techniques, providing users with insights into how decisions are made.

In addition, an AI/ML product manager must be vigilant about potential unintended consequences of the technology. They should consider the societal and individual impacts of their product and put measures in place to prevent harm. This might involve conducting risk assessments, implementing safeguards, and establishing a process for continuous monitoring and response to emerging issues.

In essence, the role of an AI/ML product manager as a guardian of ethics is crucial to ensure that AI/ML products are developed and used responsibly. The next sections will further explore how a product manager can effectively tackle these ethical considerations in their work.

Quality Assurance Advocate

Quality assurance takes on an even more pivotal role when it comes to AI/ML product management. Given that the potency and performance of AI/ML models are largely contingent upon the quality of the input data, the task of assuring data quality becomes critical. Here, the AI/ML product manager emerges as an advocate for quality assurance, dedicating resources and effort towards ensuring a high standard of data quality.

Collaboration forms a cornerstone of this endeavour. The AI/ML product manager must work closely with data engineers and data scientists to understand the data requirements for different AI/ML models. This can involve understanding the type and format of data needed, the necessary volume of data for training models effectively, and the specific characteristics that the data must possess.

Further, an AI/ML product manager should also be involved in resolving data-related issues. This may encompass a range of activities, from troubleshooting data collection errors to addressing discrepancies in the data to even mitigating bias in the dataset. By staying on top of these issues, the product manager can contribute towards the overall quality of the AI/ML models that are part of the product.

In addition to this, the AI/ML product manager is also responsible for maintaining a high standard of data quality throughout the product's lifecycle. They should establish processes and checkpoints to monitor and maintain data quality continuously. This could include setting up automated data validation checks, regularly auditing the data for accuracy and relevance, and ensuring the right data cleaning practices are in place.

Additionally, the AI/ML product manager must foster an environment that values data quality within the team. They can do so by setting clear expectations about data quality standards and fostering a culture that respects these standards. They must also ensure that data quality is communicated and understood by all stakeholders involved in the product's development and use.

In sum, an AI/ML product manager plays a crucial role as a quality assurance advocate, making sure that the data feeding into AI/ML models is of the highest quality. Ensuring data quality is not just about improving model performance – it's also about building a reliable, trustworthy product that users can depend on.

Champion of User Experience

Lastly, the AI/ML product manager is a champion of user experience. AI/ML technologies can significantly enhance user experience through personalised content, predictive features, and intelligent assistance. The AI/ML product manager must understand these capabilities and work with the UX team to integrate them into the product design.

In the chapters that follow, we'll delve deeper into each of these aspects. We'll provide a comprehensive guide to mastering the complexities and nuances of the AI/ML product management role. Along the way, we'll share insights, tips, and strategies gleaned from industry veterans and experts. We'll explore real-world case studies that illustrate the principles and practices of AI/ML product management. And we'll equip you with the tools and frameworks you need to succeed in this challenging and exciting role.

In essence, being an AI/ML product manager is about more than just managing a product; it's about envisioning the future, harnessing technology, and creating value. It's about understanding the world of AI/ML and translating it into a world of product development. And it's about striking a balance - a balance between technology and practicality, between innovation and feasibility, and between ambition and ethics.

So, as you embark on this journey, remember that the role of an AI/ML product manager is not a fixed destination but a dynamic, evolving journey. It's a journey of learning, adapting, and growing. It's a journey that challenges you, inspires you, and transforms you. And above all, it's a journey that shapes the future of products, businesses, and society.

In the world of AI/ML product management, you're not just a product manager; you're a pioneer, a trailblazer, and a changemaker. And this chapter is the first step on your path to becoming one. So, let's delve in, explore, and discover the exciting world of AI/ML product management.

As you embark on this journey, remember that mastering the role of an AI/ML product manager is not just about learning the principles and practices of product management. It's also about developing a mindset - a mindset of curiosity, open-mindedness, and perseverance. And it's about embodying a set of values - values of integrity, responsibility, and excellence.

In the end, being an AI/ML product manager is not just a profession; it's a passion, a calling, and a mission. And we're here to guide you, support you, and inspire you on this journey. Welcome to the world of AI/ML product management. Let's dive in, explore, and make a difference.

Chapter 3

Essential Skills for AI/ML Product Managers

In the rapidly-evolving landscape of AI and ML, the role of a product manager is multifaceted and challenging. This position necessitates a robust understanding of AI/ML technologies along with an array of complementary skills. Beyond this, the product manager in the AI/ML domain must also keep pace with the latest developments and trends in technology, user behaviour, and regulatory guidelines.

As the world increasingly gravitates towards an AI-first approach, the need for product managers who can navigate the complexity of this field grows. These professionals need to understand the intricacies of AI and ML and how to leverage these technologies to create compelling products that meet customer needs and align with business objectives.

If you aspire to become an AI/ML product manager, you're embarking on a path that is as challenging as rewarding. You will need to continually learn, adapt, and develop a diverse range of skills. In this chapter, we'll outline the essential skills that every aspiring AI/ML product manager must strive to cultivate.

As we traverse this landscape of requisite skills, it's crucial to note that the list we provide is not exhaustive. The world of AI/ML is dynamic, with the potential for new breakthroughs and developments at any time. As such, the skills required of an AI/ML product manager may also evolve and change over time.

With that in mind, this chapter serves as a guide to help you navigate your learning journey. The skills we discuss here are based on the current state of the industry and the collective experiences of many successful AI/ML product managers. However, as you progress in your career, you'll likely need to acquire new skills and knowledge.

Let's begin our exploration of the essential skills for an AI/ML product manager. From technical proficiencies to business acumen, from strategic thinking to interpersonal abilities - our goal is to provide you with a comprehensive understanding of what it takes to succeed in this dynamic and exciting field. As you read, consider your existing skills and how they align with the ones we discuss. Use this chapter as a roadmap for your professional development, a guide to help you evolve from an aspiring AI/ML product manager to a successful one.

In the sections that follow, we will dissect each of these skills, why they matter in the realm of AI/ML product management, and how you can go about acquiring and enhancing them. Let's dive into this exciting journey of skill-building, self-improvement, and continual learning.

1. Understanding of AI/ML Principles

The field of Artificial Intelligence and Machine Learning is full of complex concepts and intricate algorithms. But fear not, as the first and foremost skill you need as an AI/ML Product Manager is not to become a data scientist but to develop a fundamental understanding of AI/ML principles. This understanding forms the bedrock on which you can build your technical proficiency.

To navigate the realm of AI/ML product management effectively, it's essential to be comfortable with core concepts such as supervised Learning, unsupervised Learning, reinforcement learning, neural networks, and natural language processing. Having a firm grasp of these principles can serve you in numerous ways. Not only will it empower you to converse fluently with technical stakeholders, but it will also enable you to make informed decisions about the product's AI/ML features.

Supervised Learning, the most common type of machine learning, revolves around teaching machines to make predictions based on labelled data, i.e., data that comes with a known answer. Familiar examples include email spam filters and weather forecasting applications.

Unsupervised Learning, on the other hand, involves learning from unlabelled data, finding hidden patterns and structures within. This method is particularly useful in exploring vast amounts of data where human annotation would be impractical or biased.

Reinforcement Learning is a type of machine learning where an agent learns to make decisions by taking actions in an environment to maximise some notion of cumulative reward. It's the fundamental concept behind self-driving cars and recommendation systems.

Neural Networks are a set of algorithms modelled after the human brain, designed to recognise patterns. They interpret sensory data through a kind of machine perception, labelling or clustering of raw input.

Natural Language Processing (NLP) is the ability of a computer program to understand human language as it is spoken. It involves machine interpretation, generation, and translation of human language, enabling humans to interact with computers using natural sentences.

By understanding these AI/ML principles, you're equipped to assess the feasibility and appropriateness of different AI/ML approaches in the context of your product's needs. You can discern between what's possible, what's practical, and what's merely 'hype'. You'll also be better positioned to comprehend the challenges, risks, and limitations associated with various AI/ML implementations, which in turn will help you manage stakeholder expectations effectively.

In addition, a strong foundation in AI/ML principles will enable you to communicate more effectively with the technical team. You'll be able to understand their language, appreciate their challenges, and translate the technical aspects of the product into the language of business, benefits, and user value. This skill is crucial in fostering effective collaboration and ensuring alignment between different teams and stakeholders.

Finally, understanding AI/ML principles will empower you to stay abreast of the latest trends and developments in the field. AI/ML is a rapidly evolving domain, with new techniques, tools, and applications emerging all the time. By being conversant with the underlying principles, you'll be better able to comprehend and assimilate these new developments, thereby keeping your product competitive and relevant in the marketplace.

As you set out to deepen your understanding of AI/ML principles, remember that it's not about mastering every detail but about having a solid conceptual understanding. A range of resources, including online courses, books, podcasts, and professional communities, can support you in this learning journey.

In the end, the goal is to build your technical proficiency in AI/ML, not just to 'speak tech' but to 'think tech'. This means understanding how AI/ML can drive value, enhance user experience, and create a strategic advantage for your product. With this understanding, you can truly embody the role of an AI/ML product manager - a bridge between the realms of technology and

2. Data Literacy

Data, often referred to as the "new oil", plays a central role in AI/ML. Therefore, an AI/ML product manager's toolkit must include a thorough understanding of data. As such, data literacy – the ability to read, understand, create and communicate data as information – becomes an essential skill.

Understanding Data Structures

At the heart of data literacy is a solid understanding of data structures. It's crucial to comprehend the difference between structured data (which is typically numerical or categorical data that can easily be sorted and analysed) and unstructured data (such as text, images, or voice, which require more complex methods to analyse). You need to understand the basics of databases, knowing how data is stored, retrieved and organised. Familiarisation with different types of databases, such as relational databases and NoSQL databases, will help you in discussions with your technical team.

Interpreting Data Visualisations

Data visualisation is a powerful tool in the product manager's arsenal, turning raw data into easily digestible visual narratives. Knowing how to interpret data visualisations can unlock significant insights, such as user behaviours, market trends, and product performance. Whether it's a simple bar chart, a scatter plot or a complex heat map, deciphering these visualisations equips you to make evidence-based decisions.

Data Manipulation Basics

While you may not be writing SQL queries or Python scripts daily as a product manager, understanding the basics of data manipulation can be very beneficial. This knowledge will help you understand the process your technical team undergoes to turn raw data into meaningful insights. It will also allow you to do basic data exploration yourself, enhancing your understanding and control over the product's data assets.

Data Quality and Data Governance

Data quality and data governance are also critical aspects of data literacy. As an AI/ML product manager, you need to understand that the effectiveness of AI/ML algorithms is only as good as the data they feed on. Therefore, ensuring data quality, integrity, and accuracy becomes a critical task.

Data governance, on the other hand, is about managing the availability, usability, integrity, and security of data. As an AI/ML product manager, you must be aware of the best practices of data governance, the regulatory requirements, and the ethical considerations surrounding data use.

Having a solid foundation in data literacy not only enables you to navigate the technical aspects of AI/ML but also empowers you to act as a bridge between technical and non-technical stakeholders. You can translate the story that data tells into strategic insights, guiding the product's vision and roadmap. Furthermore, a high level of data literacy allows you to ask the right questions, challenge assumptions, and ensure that decisions are data-driven and not just based on intuition.

The pursuit of data literacy is an ongoing journey that will yield rich dividends in the form of improved product decision-making, more effective collaboration with technical teams, and, ultimately, a more successful AI/ML product.

3. Technical Acumen

Technical acumen, encompassing a basic understanding of programming principles, software development methodologies, and system architecture, is an integral part of the AI/ML product manager's skill set. While the role doesn't require the mastery of programming languages or the ability to write complex code, being fluent in "tech-speak" allows for efficient collaboration with the engineering team, insightful understanding of the product's technical constraints and opportunities, and effective decision-making throughout the product development process.

Programming Principles

Understanding basic programming principles is similar to learning the grammar of a language. It involves grasping concepts like variables, control flow, functions, and data structures, to name a few. Familiarity with these constructs provides a window into the developers' world, enabling you to better appreciate the challenges they face and the solutions they propose.

For an AI/ML product manager, a rudimentary understanding of the programming languages most commonly used in AI/ML applications, like Python and R, can be especially helpful. Furthermore, knowing the basics of scripting languages like SQL for database management adds another string to your technical bow.

Software Development Methodologies

Being aware of software development methodologies such as Agile, Scrum, or Waterfall can significantly enhance your effectiveness as a product manager. Understanding these methodologies, their stages, their advantages, and their trade-offs can inform your decision-making and facilitate smoother collaboration with your engineering team.

For instance, understanding Agile principles can guide you in maintaining flexibility in your product planning, enabling you to incorporate user feedback or address market changes rapidly. Similarly, understanding the concept of "sprints" in Scrum can help you in effectively planning and prioritising the product backlog.

System Architecture

A comprehension of system architecture is another cornerstone of technical acumen. Knowing how different components of your product interact and depend on each other can shape your strategic decisions regarding feature development and resource allocation.

Understanding cloud computing platforms, for example, can help you appreciate the scalability and cost implications of your product decisions. Likewise, an understanding of data architecture can be vital in discussions around data storage, processing, and security.

In conclusion, technical acumen, though not requiring a deep dive into coding or system engineering, is about understanding the language of technology sufficiently to engage in meaningful conversations with your technical counterparts and to make informed decisions regarding your product. As an AI/ML product manager, this understanding will allow you to see both the possibilities and the limitations of technology, shaping your product's direction in ways that are both visionary and grounded in technical reality.

Technical acumen is a skill that can be continually honed over time learning from your technical team, participating in relevant training, and staying updated with technology trends. As you build this skill, you'll find yourself better equipped to lead the charge in developing AI/ML products that are innovative, technically sound, and responsive to user needs.

4. Problem-Solving Skills

Problem-solving skills represent a cornerstone in the complex and often nebulous realm of AI/ML product management. As a manager, you'll frequently be confronted with multifaceted issues and challenges that demand a blend of creativity, analytical prowess, and pragmatism. Developing a robust problem-solving mindset is thus an indispensable asset.

Analytical Reasoning

In a world brimming with data, the ability to interpret and derive actionable insights from it is a key facet of problem-solving. This includes understanding data, recognising patterns, extracting key insights, and applying these to make informed decisions. For an AI/ML product manager, analytical reasoning becomes all the more critical because of the data-driven nature of AI/ML technologies. You'll be required to scrutinise data quality, investigate model outputs, and discern potential biases, making analytical reasoning an essential skill.

Creative Thinking

Problem-solving isn't confined solely to analytical prowess; it also requires creative thinking. Creative thinking engenders innovative solutions to problems and encourages 'out-of-the-box' thinking. This might involve brainstorming new features, imagining fresh applications of AI/ML, or devising novel strategies to improve user engagement. In an industry where differentiation can be pivotal, the capacity to think differently is invaluable.

Structural Approach

While analytical reasoning and creative thinking form the backbone of problem-solving, the ability to approach problems systematically is what binds these elements together. This typically involves defining the problem clearly, breaking it down into manageable components, formulating hypotheses, testing these hypotheses, and finally, implementing and reviewing solutions. This approach not only facilitates effective problem-solving but also helps communicate your thought process to others, fostering collaboration and mutual understanding.

Critical Evaluation

Finally, the skill of critical evaluation is an integral part of problem-solving. As an AI/ML product manager, you must be adept at questioning assumptions, testing validity, and weighing the pros and cons of different solutions. This involves understanding potential pitfalls of AI/ML technologies, like data privacy issues or model biases, and ensuring these considerations are factored into your decision-making process.

In conclusion, problem-solving skills, combining analytical reasoning, creative thinking, a structured approach, and critical evaluation, form a critical competency for an AI/ML product manager. It's a journey of continuously honing these skills, experimenting, learning from successes and failures, and nurturing a curious, open-minded perspective.

This amalgamation of skills allows an AI/ML product manager to navigate the intricate maze of product development, uncovering solutions that align with user needs, business goals, and the ever-evolving landscape of AI/ML technology. With these skills in your repertoire, you'll be equipped to tackle the exciting challenges that AI/ML product management offers, steering your product towards success.

5. Strategic Thinking

Strategic thinking in the context of AI/ML isn't about grasping at the next flashy technology trend. It's about taking a structured and long-term approach to leverage AI/ML technologies to further business goals, outmanoeuvre competitors, and generate sustainable value for users. In the fast-paced world of AI/ML, where technologies are continually evolving, strategic thinking is what keeps a product grounded yet forward-looking.

Seeing the Whole Chessboard

Strategic thinking begins with a broad perspective. This means understanding not just your product but also the broader ecosystem within which it operates. How does your product fit into the company's overall portfolio? What are the market trends that could impact your product? How might advancements in AI/ML technologies disrupt your industry? These are the types of questions you need to ponder.

Translating Strategy into Action

A key part of strategic thinking involves translating high-level strategy into concrete actions and decisions. This means not only understanding the company's strategic objectives but also determining how AI/ML can be used to achieve these objectives. It could involve implementing AI to streamline operations, using ML to personalise user experience, or leveraging AI/ML to drive innovation and open up new markets.

Thinking Long-Term

AI/ML technologies are constantly evolving, and what's cutting-edge today might be obsolete tomorrow. Strategic thinking, therefore, involves maintaining a long-term outlook. This includes keeping an eye on the technological horizon to anticipate future trends and developments. It also means building scalability and adaptability into your product, so it can evolve and grow as AI/ML technologies advance.

Balancing Risk and Reward

Strategic thinking also involves assessing and balancing risk and reward. AI/ML technologies can offer significant rewards, including operational efficiency, competitive advantage, and customer satisfaction. However, they also carry risks, such as security vulnerabilities, regulatory compliance issues, and ethical dilemmas. Balancing these potential rewards and risks requires careful thought and judgement.

Incorporating Stakeholder Perspectives

Finally, strategic thinking entails considering various stakeholder perspectives. This includes understanding the needs and concerns of users, the interests of the company, the requirements of regulatory bodies, and the expectations of society at large. By incorporating these diverse perspectives, you can build a more robust and holistic strategy.

In sum, strategic thinking is a critical skill for an AI/ML product manager.

It requires seeing the whole chessboard, translating strategy into action, thinking long-term, balancing risk and reward, and incorporating stakeholder perspectives. By honing this skill, you can ensure that AI/ML is used strategically and responsibly, delivering sustainable value to users and the business.

Remember, strategic thinking is not a one-and-done exercise but a continuous process. It's about regularly revisiting and updating your strategy as new information and insights emerge. It's about being nimble and flexible, ready to pivot when necessary while keeping your eyes firmly on the long-term vision. This is the art and science of strategic thinking in AI/ML product management.

6. Ethical Awareness

The increasing ubiquity of AI/ML applications has made ethical awareness indispensable in the realm of product management. Ethical issues tied to AI/ML range from data privacy and fairness to transparency and accountability. As an AI/ML product manager, the mantle of responsibility lies heavily on your shoulders to ensure these considerations are part and parcel of the development lifecycle, shaping both the inception and execution of the product.

The Data Privacy Paradox

AI/ML technologies are voracious consumers of data. From recommender systems to predictive models, these technologies rely on vast volumes of data to operate effectively. However, this presents a paradox. On the one hand, more data can improve the efficiency and accuracy of AI/ML models; on the other, it raises serious concerns about user privacy.

It's incumbent upon an AI/ML product manager to understand and navigate this tension. You'll need to be conversant in data privacy laws such as GDPR in Europe and CCPA in California, along with understanding the broader societal expectations around data privacy. This knowledge must then inform the product's data strategies and policies.

Fairness and Bias

AI/ML models learn from data. If the data contains biases, the models will likely perpetuate and potentially amplify these biases. This can lead to unfair outcomes and could cause considerable harm, depending on the application of AI/ML technology.

An AI/ML product manager must ensure that fairness is factored into the design and implementation of the product. This might involve scrutinising training data for biases, testing AI/ML models for fair outcomes, and working with AI/ML engineers to apply techniques that mitigate bias.

Transparency and Interpretability

Many AI/ML models, particularly deep learning models, are considered "black boxes". This means it's difficult, if not impossible, to understand how they arrive at their decisions. This lack of transparency can make it hard for users to trust the product and poses challenges for accountability.

As an AI/ML product manager, it's essential to advocate for transparency and interpretability. This could mean prioritising interpretable models over black box models, or it could involve developing features that explain the model's decisions to users in a clear and understandable way.

Ethical Leadership

Beyond these specific issues, an AI/ML product manager must also embody ethical leadership. This means advocating for ethical considerations in product discussions and decision-making, fostering a culture of ethical awareness within the product team, and holding oneself and others accountable for the ethical implications of the product.

By cultivating ethical awareness, you can contribute to developing AI/ML technologies that are innovative and effective but also responsible and trustworthy.

7. Communication Skills - The Listening Leader

A crucial but often overlooked aspect of communication is the ability to listen effectively. Listening is about more than just hearing the words that someone is saying. It's about genuinely understanding their perspective, acknowledging their concerns, and validating their contributions. In the world of AI/ML product management, where complex, novel ideas are being discussed and debated continuously, the importance of effective listening cannot be overstated.

Being a good listener means resisting the urge to interrupt or prematurely propose solutions while others are speaking. It's about maintaining an open mind, free from preconceptions, and being willing to change your point of view based on the information you receive. As a product manager, your role involves balancing a myriad of perspectives, including those of users, engineers, designers, and business stakeholders. By honing your listening skills, you ensure that these voices are heard, respected, and factored into the decision-making process.

Mastering the Art of Simplicity

While there's a natural inclination to 'speak the same language' as your audience, this often leads to the assumption that complex language should be used with technical stakeholders and simplified language with non-technical stakeholders. This could not be further from the truth. No matter who your audience is, clear and straightforward communication is paramount. In a field as complex as AI/ML, it's easy to get lost in the jargon and technical details. However, the mark of a skilled communicator, and by extension, a competent product manager, is the ability to distil complex concepts into simple, digestible terms.

Bridging the Gap

In AI/ML product management, you will often find yourself acting as a bridge between the technical and non-technical realms. It is in this capacity that your communication skills will be most rigorously tested. On the one hand, you need to translate the business requirements, and user needs into technical language for the engineers and data scientists. On the other hand, you need to interpret the possibilities and limitations of AI/ML technology for the benefit of business stakeholders and users.

Achieving this balance requires a deep understanding of both sides of the divide. You should be well-versed in AI/ML principles, but you should also have a firm grasp of the business context and user needs. Above all, you should be able to empathise with both sets of stakeholders, understand their perspectives and use this understanding to facilitate effective communication.

The Power of Visual Communication

Another vital aspect of communication in AI/ML product management is the ability to use visual tools effectively. Diagrams, flowcharts, and other visual aids can be incredibly useful for explaining complex AI/ML concepts or workflows. By developing your skills in visual communication, you can make your explanations clearer and more engaging, further enhancing your effectiveness as a communicator.

In summary, effective communication is a cornerstone of successful AI/ML product management. It requires listening attentively, communicating simply and clearly, bridging the gap between technical and non-technical stakeholders, and using visual tools effectively. By cultivating these skills, you can facilitate understanding, foster collaboration, and drive the successful development of AI/ML products.

8. Project Management

In the bustling, dynamic landscape of AI/ML, product managers often find themselves walking a fine line. While their core role lies in setting the vision and strategy for the product, aligning stakeholders, and defining the product roadmap, they also inevitably grapple with aspects of project management. However, it is imperative to recognise that while there may be overlaps, project management and product management are distinct roles, each with its unique responsibilities and objectives.

Understanding Project Management: A Useful Tool

Project management involves planning, coordinating, and overseeing specific tasks to accomplish a specific goal within a stipulated timeframe. It is more tactical and closely tied to schedules, timelines, and resource allocation. In contrast, product management is broader in scope and more strategic, dealing with a product's entire lifecycle, from conception to retirement.

That said, understanding project management methodologies and tools can benefit an AI/ML product manager. It enables you to have informed discussions with the project managers, understands the intricacies of execution and timeframes better, and foresee potential hurdles in the implementation of your product strategy.

Collaborating with Project Managers

In many organisations, product managers and project managers work hand in hand, their roles intersecting yet complementary. As an AI/ML product manager, your primary responsibility lies in defining what needs to be done – the 'what', 'why', and 'for whom'. On the other hand, project managers are typically responsible for the 'how', 'when', and 'who'. They are tasked with determining how to achieve the product goals, when tasks need to be completed, and who should execute them.

A positive, collaborative relationship with project managers is, therefore, paramount. You need to provide clear, well-defined requirements and priorities and trust the project managers to determine the best way to achieve them. Mutual respect, open communication, and a shared understanding of the product vision and goals can foster a productive working relationship between you and the project managers.

Adopting a Project Management Mindset

While the execution of project management tasks may not fall within the realm of your responsibilities, adopting a project management mindset can be advantageous. This means understanding the importance of timelines, recognising the constraints of resources, and appreciating the intricacies of task scheduling and risk management.

This mindset can aid you in setting more realistic goals, making more informed strategic decisions, and communicating more effectively with both the project managers and the development team.

In conclusion, an AI/ML product manager must possess a robust understanding of project management principles. This knowledge aids in setting realistic expectations, fostering better collaboration with project managers, and bridging the gap between the strategic vision and the tactical execution of product development. Remember, while you may not be managing the project, understanding the project's ins and outs is fundamental to successful product management in the complex world of AI/ML.

9. Customer-Centricity

The importance of a customer-centric approach can hardly be overstated in any business domain, but in the ever-evolving world of AI/ML, it assumes even greater significance. Navigating this complex landscape requires a meticulous understanding of not only the intricate workings of the technology but also the people who use it. At the core of every successful AI/ML product lies a deep and authentic focus on the customer. As an AI/ML product manager, it is incumbent upon you to grasp the nuances of the customer's needs, empathise with their challenges, and perpetually strive to deliver a product that offers value.

Understanding the Customer: The Starting Point

At the heart of customer-centricity is the ability to understand the customer deeply. This understanding extends beyond knowing who your customers are to include what they want, why they want it, and how they will interact with your product. It involves getting under the skin of your customer personas and grasping the problems they face that your product can solve.

In the context of AI/ML, this understanding must extend to how customers will interact with AI/ML features. How will these features make their lives easier, more efficient, or more enjoyable? How will these interactions fit into their current workflows or routines? Understanding these aspects is fundamental to developing an AI/ML product that truly meets customer needs.

Empathy: A Vital Tool in the Product Manager's Kit

Empathy is a potent tool in the customer-centric product manager's toolkit. It involves truly feeling the customers' pain points, frustrations, and desires. An empathetic product manager can put themselves in the customers' shoes and view the world from their perspective.

With AI/ML technologies, empathy becomes even more critical due to the technologies' abstract and sometimes intimidating nature. Not all customers may be comfortable with or understanding of these technologies. Being able to empathise with their concerns, fears, and confusion can help create an AI/ML product that feels accessible, user-friendly, and trustworthy.

The Relentless Pursuit of Value

Every product exists to provide value to its customers, and AI/ML products are no different. As a product manager, your role is to consistently question, probe, and challenge to ensure your product is delivering maximum value. This means continually gathering and analysing customer feedback, conducting user testing, and being unafraid to pivot when necessary.

In the AI/ML space, where novelty can often overshadow utility, maintaining a relentless focus on value is crucial. It's easy to get caught up in the potential of AI/ML technologies, but the most successful product managers never lose sight of the fact that every feature, no matter how advanced or exciting, must provide real, tangible value to the customer.

In conclusion, a customer-centric approach is a cornerstone of successful AI/ML product management. This approach is anchored in a deep understanding of the customer, a strong sense of empathy, and a continual commitment to delivering value. These are the keys to creating an AI/ML product that not only wows customers with its technological prowess but also wins their loyalty by genuinely meeting their needs.

10. Lifelong Learning

AI/ML is a rapidly evolving field, and it's crucial to stay updated with the latest developments. This requires a commitment to lifelong learning and a curiosity about new technologies and possibilities.

By cultivating these skills, you'll be well-equipped to navigate the exciting world of AI/ML product management. Each of these skills complements the others, and together, they create a well-rounded AI/ML product manager.

Keep in mind that this isn't a checklist to be completed overnight. Rather, it's a roadmap for continual development and growth. With every step you take on this journey, you'll become a more capable and confident AI/ML product manager. So, start where you are, use what you have, and do what you can. With persistence, patience, and passion, you're sure to succeed.

11 The Power of Leadership: Inspiring and Unifying Your Team

In the intricate and dynamic world of AI/ML product management, the onus of guiding a cross-functional team towards a unified vision lies on the shoulders of the product manager. As such, leadership skills are not merely desirable—they're a prerequisite for success. An effective AI/ML product manager is a beacon, illuminating the path for the team and inspiring them to march towards their common goals. Leadership in this context is not about wielding authority; it's about harnessing influence, practising empathy, and fostering a culture of collaboration.

Leadership through Influence: From Vision to Reality

Influence is a critical component of leadership. As an AI/ML product manager, you're expected to steer the direction of the product, often without direct authority over the team.

This is where the power of influence comes into play. You need to earn the respect of your team, stakeholders, and superiors through your deep understanding of the product, market, and, most importantly, the customer. Your influence will be the driving force that helps convert the product vision into a tangible reality.

The application of AI/ML technologies opens up a realm of possibilities that can revolutionise the product landscape. However, the novelty and complexity associated with these technologies can also generate ambiguity and resistance. It is here that your influential leadership becomes vital. You should be adept at selling the vision, encouraging your team to embrace change, and assisting them in navigating through any hurdles that arise during the product development journey.

Embracing Empathy: The Human Touch in Leadership

In the race to stay ahead of the AI/ML curve, it is easy to overlook the human element of product management. An effective leader recognises that behind every product, there are people—people who develop it, market it, sell it, buy it, and use it. Understanding and empathising with these people is an essential quality of an AI/ML product manager.

Empathy is not just about understanding others' perspectives; it is also about acknowledging their feelings, appreciating their efforts, and respecting their opinions.

Your ability to empathise with your team, stakeholders, and customers will directly impact your effectiveness as a leader. This ability will also enable you to build an inclusive product that meets the diverse needs of your customer base.

Facilitating Collaboration: The Catalyst for Success

A successful AI/ML product is the result of various elements working in harmony—be it the data engineers ensuring the quality of data, the AI/ML engineers developing robust algorithms, the UX designers creating intuitive interfaces, or the marketing team crafting compelling narratives. As a product manager, you are the orchestrator of this harmonious symphony.

Your leadership should foster an environment where collaboration thrives. You should manage conflicts constructively, encourage open communication, and ensure everyone's views are heard and valued. Your ability to facilitate collaboration can significantly accelerate decision-making processes and enhance the overall effectiveness of your team.

Leadership in AI/ML product management is a complex yet fulfilling responsibility. It is a delicate balancing act that requires you to be a visionary and a pragmatist, a strategist and an executor, an influencer and a listener. By nurturing these leadership skills, you will be well-positioned to guide your team and product towards success, no matter how challenging the AI/ML landscape may be.

12. Knowledge of Regulatory Environment

The rapid rise of AI/ML technologies has brought to the fore a series of regulatory considerations. Indeed, we find ourselves in an era where understanding the legal and regulatory landscape is no longer a mere accessory but a fundamental part of an AI/ML product manager's toolkit. With regulations like the General Data Protection Regulation (GDPR) in Europe and guidelines from bodies such as the Federal Trade Commission (FTC) in the United States, the product development process is increasingly subjected to regulatory scrutiny.

Regulatory Knowledge: A Shield against Legal Pitfalls

Understanding these regulations isn't merely about avoiding penalties or the wrath of regulatory bodies; it's about protecting your company's reputation, maintaining customer trust, and ensuring sustainable product growth. Ignorance of the law, as they say, is no defence. Knowledge of the regulatory environment acts as a shield, protecting your product from potential legal complications that could hinder its development or deployment.

Navigating the regulatory landscape requires one to be constantly vigilant and adaptable, as regulations often evolve alongside advancements in technology. As an AI/ML product manager, you must keep abreast of the latest changes, anticipate future amendments, and understand their implications for your product.

GDPR and Beyond: The Global Regulatory Environment

While GDPR has become a well-known acronym in businesses handling European data, it's important to remember that the regulatory environment extends far beyond this single regulation. From the California Consumer Privacy Act (CCPA) to China's Cybersecurity Law and beyond, regulations vary widely based on geographic location. Having a working knowledge of the regulatory landscape in the areas you operate is imperative to ensuring compliance and avoiding hefty fines or legal complications.

However, understanding the intricacies of these regulations is only part of the challenge. The real task lies in translating these regulatory requirements into concrete actions within your product's development lifecycle. This involves working closely with legal teams, data governance teams, and technical teams to ensure your product remains compliant at every stage, from data collection to data processing and storage.

Regulation as an Opportunity

It's easy to view the ever-increasing regulatory scrutiny as a hurdle. However, it's far more productive—and indeed, accurate—to see it as an opportunity. Compliance with regulations is a demonstration of your product's credibility, reliability, and commitment to user safety and privacy. It's a chance to instil confidence in your stakeholders, differentiate your product from competitors, and ultimately increase market trust in your product.

Moreover, these regulations often serve as a guiding light, illuminating the path to ethical AI/ML practices. By following these guidelines, we can ensure our technologies are developed and used in a manner that respects user rights and promotes fair, transparent AI/ML practices.

In conclusion, the importance of understanding the regulatory environment in AI/ML cannot be overstated. It's an essential skill that will empower you to navigate the legal complexities, ensure regulatory compliance, and ultimately, safeguard your product's success in the ever-evolving AI/ML landscape.

13. Commercial Acumen

AI and Machine Learning are not just mere buzzwords in the modern tech landscape; they are powerful tools that have the potential to transform businesses, disrupt industries, and redefine the way we interact with the world around us. However, while the allure of AI/ML is undeniable, their application isn't a guaranteed ticket to success. The bridge that connects AI/ML technologies to profitability is paved with astute commercial acumen.

Why Commercial Acumen?

Simply put, commercial acumen is the ability to understand and navigate the marketplace, your competition, and your business model to maximise profitability. As an AI/ML product manager, your responsibilities extend beyond the realm of technicalities. You need to be commercially savvy, able to evaluate the commercial viability of product ideas and understand how these contribute to the company's bottom line.

The landscape of AI/ML is a fascinating yet challenging terrain, brimming with opportunities yet fraught with uncertainty. Thus, commercial acumen becomes indispensable, allowing you to identify market opportunities, discern potential risks, and devise strategies that ensure your product's long-term viability and profitability.

Making Business Sense of AI/ML

It begins with understanding your market and competition. With AI/ML rapidly gaining traction, markets are becoming increasingly saturated, with competitors continuously pushing the boundaries of innovation. In such a dynamic environment, a sound understanding of the market trends and competitive landscape can help position your product favourably and capitalise on opportunities that others may overlook.

However, commercial acumen doesn't stop at understanding your external environment; it extends to internal understanding. How does your product fit within the company's overall business strategy? What role does it play in your business model? What value does it bring to your organisation? These are questions that you, as an AI/ML product manager, must strive to answer.

Driving Commercial Success with AI/ML

But it's not enough to merely understand the commercial aspects; it's equally crucial to use that understanding to drive your product's commercial success. This involves evaluating the commercial viability of product ideas, making financially informed decisions, and consistently assessing your product's performance against commercial KPIs.

Moreover, commercial acumen involves championing the customer. After all, at the heart of any profitable venture lies satisfied customers. Understanding their needs, their pain points, and how your product can provide value to them is a critical part of driving your product's commercial success.

In conclusion, as an AI/ML product manager, having a robust technical foundation is undoubtedly crucial. Still, it's your commercial acumen that will turn that technical potential into commercial success. By developing a keen understanding of the market, competition, and your business model, you can ensure your product not only leverages the power of AI/ML but also contributes to the company's bottom line, driving the transition from AI to ROI.

14. Resilience and Adaptability

In the fast-paced world of technology, the only constant is change.

This is especially true in the realm of AI/ML product management, where rapid advancements, shifting user expectations, and evolving regulatory landscapes continually redefine the status quo. The ability to weather these storms, to persist amidst challenges, and adapt to shifting circumstances, is encapsulated in two key attributes: resilience and adaptability.

Resilience: The Bedrock of Success

Resilience refers to the ability to bounce back from adversity, maintain your composure in the face of pressure, and keep moving forward despite setbacks. In the world of AI/ML product management, adversity can come in many forms. It could be a failed product launch, a technical glitch that compromises your product's performance, or even negative customer feedback that undermines your product's reputation.

However, it is in these moments of adversity where resilience shines the brightest. It enables you to take these setbacks in your stride, learn from them, and use them as stepping stones to success. It ensures that you remain committed to your vision, persistent in your efforts, and steadfast on your path, even when the odds seem stacked against you.

Adaptability: Your Beacon in the Storm

While resilience enables you to weather the storm, adaptability equips you to navigate through it. Adaptability is about being flexible in your approach, open to new ideas, and quick to adjust to changing circumstances. As an AI/ML product manager, this might mean pivoting your product strategy in response to market changes, adopting new technologies to enhance your product's capabilities, or revising your product's design based on user feedback.

Adaptability is not about blindly following trends or impulsively jumping onto the next big thing. It's about having the acumen to discern what changes are worth embracing and having the agility to implement these changes efficiently. It's about staying ahead of the curve, anticipating changes before they occur, and continually evolving your product to meet the ever-changing needs of your users.

Resilience and Adaptability: The Dynamic Duo

While resilience and adaptability are powerful on their own, they are at their most potent when coupled together. Resilience provides you with the strength to persist amidst adversity, while adaptability equips you with the flexibility to navigate through change. Together, they empower you to not just survive the tumultuous world of AI/ML product management but to thrive within it.

In conclusion, as an AI/ML product manager, your journey will undoubtedly be marked by waves of change, unexpected challenges, and intense pressures.

However, by cultivating resilience and adaptability, you can ensure that you remain unfazed by these adversities, ready to adapt to the evolving landscape, and steadfast on your path to success. After all, as Charles Darwin once said, "It is not the strongest of the species that survives, nor the most intelligent; it is the one most adaptable to change." In the world of AI/ML product management, this wisdom holds more truth than ever.

15. Networking Skills

Building relationships with other professionals in the AI/ML industry can open up opportunities for collaboration, learning, and growth. Networking skills can also be invaluable when it comes to hiring a team, finding mentors, or navigating organisational politics.

In closing, it's essential to note that the journey of developing these skills is not a linear one, and neither is it a race. Each individual brings unique strengths and experiences to the table and may find some skills more intuitive to master than others. That's perfectly fine. Embrace your unique journey, and instead of comparing yourself with others, focus on becoming a better version of yourself each day.

At the same time, remember that skills are not static. They evolve with experience, and they can always be improved. So, even once you've become an AI/ML product manager, continue to invest in your skill development. Take courses, attend workshops, read books, seek feedback, and constantly challenge yourself to learn and grow.

As Albert Einstein once said, "Once you stop learning, you start dying." In the ever-evolving world of AI/ML, this rings truer than ever. So, embrace learning as a lifelong journey, and remember that every step you take on this journey brings you one step closer to becoming a successful AI/ML product manager.

Ultimately, the most important skill for an AI/ML product manager is the ability to blend the technical with the practical, the strategic with the tactical, and the innovative with the feasible. This requires a delicate balance of hard and soft skills, a deep understanding of both technology and people and the vision to see beyond the present and into the future.

As you continue to develop these skills and take on the challenges of AI/ML product management, remember that you're not alone on this journey. Whether it's mentors, peers, or books like this one, there are countless resources and allies out there to help you succeed. So, keep learning, keep growing, and keep pushing the boundaries of what's possible. Your journey as an AI/ML product manager is just beginning, and the future is bright.

Part II

Preparing for Your AI/ML PM Interview

Entering the fray of the AI/ML product management job market can seem daunting, especially given the rapidly evolving landscape of AI/ML technologies. Yet, with the right preparation, you can not only survive this challenging process but truly excel. This part of the book will guide you through the essential steps of preparing for your AI/ML PM interview, helping you to stand out in the competitive crowd and get one step closer to landing your dream role.

Chapter 4: Understanding the AI/ML PM Job Market

Before you even begin to tailor your resume or prepare for interviews, you need to have a firm grasp of the AI/ML PM job market. This includes understanding the key players in the industry, the emerging trends, the different types of roles available, and the expectations and requirements of these roles. This knowledge will enable you to target your job search effectively, ensuring you're applying for roles that align with your skills, interests, and career aspirations.

We'll also look at the evolution of the AI/ML PM job market, giving you a historical perspective that can help you predict and prepare for future trends. After all, the world of AI/ML is constantly changing, and staying ahead of the curve can give you a competitive edge.

Chapter 5: Tailoring Your Resume and Portfolio

In a sea of applicants, your resume and portfolio are your first opportunity to make an impression. This chapter will provide you with practical tips and strategies for tailoring your resume and portfolio to AI/ML PM roles.
We'll discuss how to highlight your relevant experiences, how to showcase your AI/ML knowledge, and how to

demonstrate the essential skills we discussed in the previous section. We'll also discuss the role of online portfolios and how you can leverage them to showcase your work in a more dynamic and engaging way.

Chapter 6: Effective Networking Strategies

Networking can be a powerful tool in your job search, opening up opportunities for mentorship, collaboration, and even job opportunities. In this chapter, we'll cover the strategies for effective networking in the AI/ML industry, both online and offline.

We'll discuss how to approach informational interviews, how to leverage social media, and how to engage with the AI/ML community through events and organizations. We'll also discuss the importance of building and maintaining relationships over time, ensuring that your network is a resource you can draw upon throughout your career.

Chapter 7: Decoding the Job Description

A job description is more than just a list of responsibilities and requirements - it's a window into the company's priorities, culture, and expectations. Learning how to decode a job description can give you valuable insights that can inform your application and interview preparation.

In this chapter, we'll delve into how to decipher key details from job descriptions, such as the specific AI/ML technologies the company uses, the team structure, the product lifecycle stage, and the broader business context. This will enable you to tailor your application and interview responses more effectively, demonstrating that you're qualified and a good fit for the role.

As you progress through these chapters, remember that preparation is a process, not an event. It requires time, effort, and perseverance. Yet, the investment is well worth it. After all, as the old adage goes, "Luck is what happens when preparation meets opportunity." So, roll up your sleeves, delve into the process, and make your own luck in the AI/ML PM job market.

Chapter 4

Understanding the AI/ML PM Job Market

Artificial Intelligence (AI) and Machine Learning (ML) – are two technological marvels that have transfigured the face of the modern era, permeating the very fabric of our daily lives. From predictive text and voice-activated virtual assistants to fraud detection systems and autonomous vehicles, the implications of AI and ML are colossal. Amidst this revolution, an emerging role has risen to prominence - the AI/ML Product Manager.

The Growing Demand for AI/ML PMs

The demand for AI/ML product managers has skyrocketed in recent years. As more industries realise the transformative potential of AI/ML technologies, the need for proficient professionals who can steer these products from ideation to execution has become paramount. Consequently, the job market is rife with opportunities for those who can effectively navigate this burgeoning frontier.

However, the AI/ML PM job market is not just burgeoning; it's diverse. From tech giants and leading-edge start-ups to traditional sectors like finance, healthcare, and retail - the applicability of AI/ML transcends industry boundaries. Consequently, the type and nature of roles available to AI/ML PMs are richly varied.

Understanding the Landscape

The AI/ML PM job market is a complex landscape that requires careful navigation. It's marked by rapid technological advancements, evolving role definitions, and increasing regulatory scrutiny. Therefore, to successfully navigate this landscape, you must understand the forces that shape it.

Technological advancements are continuously pushing the boundaries of what's possible with AI/ML, creating new opportunities and challenges. Staying updated with these trends can help you identify emerging opportunities and equip yourself with the skills required to seize them.

The role of an AI/ML PM is not set in stone; it's dynamic and influenced by factors like the company's size, culture, and the industry it operates in. Understanding these nuances can help you find a role that aligns with your skills, interests, and career aspirations.

Lastly, the increasing regulatory scrutiny of AI/ML technologies has made regulatory compliance an essential aspect of AI/ML product management. Familiarising yourself with the regulatory landscape can help you anticipate potential legal hurdles and ensure that your product meets all necessary regulations.

Positioning Yourself for Success

With a robust understanding of the AI/ML PM job market, you are better equipped to position yourself for success. This involves identifying your strengths and weaknesses, acquiring the necessary skills, and building a compelling narrative that highlights your suitability for the role.

Remember, the AI/ML PM job market, while promising, is also competitive. Hence, standing out from the crowd requires not just hard skills but also soft skills like communication, leadership, and adaptability.

In conclusion, the AI/ML PM job market, with its vast potential and diverse opportunities, stands as an inviting frontier for those ready to ride the wave of the AI/ML revolution. Understanding this landscape, its nuances, and the forces shaping it forms the bedrock of your journey towards becoming a successful AI/ML product manager. As you step onto this frontier, remember: success favours the prepared. Equip yourself with knowledge, arm yourself with skills, and the world of AI/ML product management will be yours to conquer.

A. Key Players in the Industry

The first layer of understanding the AI/ML PM job market involves identifying and understanding the key players in the industry. The landscape is diverse, from tech giants like

Google, Microsoft, and Amazon, which have dedicated AI research and development arms, to AI-focused startups and companies in traditional industries incorporating AI/ML into their operations.

It's crucial to understand the role and impact of these different players, as each offers unique opportunities and challenges. For instance, working in AI at a tech giant may offer resources and reach that smaller companies can't match but may come with higher competition and bureaucracy. On the other hand, a startup might provide more hands-on experience and decision-making authority but with increased risk and uncertainty.

B. Emerging Trends

Keeping abreast of the emerging trends in AI/ML can provide you with valuable insights into where the job market may be heading. This includes technological trends, such as the rise of explainable AI and the use of reinforcement learning, as well as industry trends, like the increasing focus on ethical AI and AI governance.

Understanding these trends can help you anticipate the skills and knowledge that will be in demand in the future and position yourself as a forward-thinking candidate. Furthermore, showcasing your knowledge of these trends during the application process demonstrates your commitment to staying up-to-date in the rapidly evolving AI/ML field.

C. Types of Roles

Another key aspect of understanding the AI/ML PM job market is recognising the variety of roles available. While the title of 'AI/ML Product Manager' might be self-explanatory, the specifics of the role can vary widely depending on the industry, company size, product stage, and specific AI/ML technologies in use.

For example, some roles may require a strong technical background with a deep understanding of specific AI/ML algorithms and technologies. Others may be more business-focused, requiring the ability to translate AI/ML capabilities into strategic business advantages. Still, others might be more user-oriented, necessitating a strong understanding of user experience and design thinking.

By understanding the breadth of roles available, you can more effectively target your job search to roles that align with your skills, interests, and career aspirations.

D. Role Expectations and Requirements

In addition to understanding the types of roles available, it's important to understand the expectations and requirements of these roles. This includes technical skills, such as proficiency in AI/ML algorithms and tools; the business skills, like strategic thinking and commercial acumen; and the interpersonal skills, such as leadership and communication.

It's also crucial to understand the expectations around experience. While some roles may require extensive experience in AI/ML or product management, others may be more open to candidates with transferable skills and a demonstrated ability to learn quickly.

Understanding these expectations and requirements can help you gauge your fit for different roles and identify areas where you may need to further develop your skills or gain additional experience.

E. Evolution of the AI/ML PM Job Market

Finally, to fully understand the AI/ML PM job market, it's useful to consider its evolution. The field of AI/ML has seen exponential growth in the last decade, and this has significantly impacted the job market. Roles that didn't exist a decade ago are now in high demand, and the pace of change doesn't seem to be slowing down.

The progression of AI/ML has not only brought forth an array of new roles but also new challenges. For instance, the increasing use of AI/ML in sensitive areas like healthcare or finance has led to growing concerns around privacy, security, and ethical use of AI. This has subsequently led to a demand for AI/ML professionals who possess technical prowess and a robust understanding of the ethical implications and regulatory constraints.

Furthermore, there's been an observable shift in the demand for AI/ML talent. Initially, there was a significant demand for researchers and engineers who could develop and implement sophisticated AI/ML algorithms. While these roles are still crucial and in demand, there is an increasing need for professionals who can bridge the gap between these technical experts and the wider business. This is where the role of the AI/ML Product Manager comes into play, ensuring that the AI/ML technologies developed are aligned with business needs and create real-world impact.

The evolution of the AI/ML PM job market also serves as a reminder of the need for continuous learning and adaptation in this field. With the pace of technological progress, the job market is continually evolving, and the skills and knowledge that are in demand today may be different from those needed in the future. As an AI/ML PM, it's important to embrace this fluidity and commit to ongoing learning and development.

Closing Thoughts

Understanding the AI/ML PM job market is not a one-off task but an ongoing process. As the field of AI/ML continues to evolve and grow, so too will the job market. Staying informed about the key players, emerging trends, types of roles, role expectations, and the evolution of the job market is crucial for your career progression.

Remember, knowledge is power. By developing a thorough understanding of the AI/ML PM job market, you can more effectively navigate your job search and career progression, make informed decisions, and set yourself up for success in this exciting and dynamic field.

In the upcoming chapters, we'll delve deeper into how to tailor your resume and portfolio, the strategies for effective networking, and decoding job descriptions – all aimed at equipping you to shine in the AI/ML PM job market. The journey may seem challenging, but remember that every great journey begins with a single step. This understanding of the job market is that crucial first stride towards your goal of becoming an AI/ML Product Manager.

Chapter 5

Crafting an Impactful AI/ML PM Resume

In the sprawling digital landscape of the 21st century, your resume remains the most vital tool in your arsenal for making a strong first impression. It is not just a list of skills and experiences; it is an extension of your professional persona, a testament to your potential, and the first step on your journey from candidate to AI/ML Product Manager. The importance of crafting an impactful resume, therefore, cannot be overstated.

Navigating the AI/ML PM Resume Landscape

Designing a resume for an AI/ML PM role involves more than just curating a list of qualifications and experiences. It necessitates a keen understanding of the AI/ML landscape, the expectations of potential employers, and the unique challenges of representing yourself on paper.

The first hurdle is understanding what potential employers are looking for in an AI/ML PM. While the precise requirements vary from company to company, there are common threads. These include an understanding of AI/ML principles, technical acumen, data literacy, strategic thinking, and, importantly, a blend of soft skills like communication, leadership, and problem-solving.

Translating Skills into Success Stories

The key to crafting a compelling AI/ML PM resume lies in your ability to translate these skills and experiences into success stories. This involves moving beyond simply listing qualifications and, instead, narrating your professional journey in a way that highlights your aptitude for the AI/ML PM role.

Let's consider data literacy, for example. Instead of merely stating, "Proficient in data analysis," delve into how you've used this skill to drive success. Did your data analysis lead to a vital business insight? Did it inform a strategic decision? Share these stories to provide a tangible demonstration of your capabilities.

The Power of Personalisation

In the race to stand out, personalisation is your most potent ally. It involves tailoring your resume to each role, researching the company, understanding its culture and values, and reflecting these in your application.

Personalisation also extends to the format of your resume. Use a clear, concise structure that allows the reader to navigate your professional journey easily. Highlight key skills and achievements, and ensure your most important experiences are prominent. Remember, your resume should be a reflection of you - unique, memorable, and impactful.

The Art of Being Authentic

As you weave the narrative of your professional journey, remember the art of being authentic. It's easy to fall into the trap of exaggerating or embellishing your skills and experiences. However, authenticity has a resonance that can't be mimicked. Be truthful about your experiences, your strengths, and even your weaknesses.

In conclusion, crafting an impactful AI/ML PM resume is a delicate balance of understanding the job landscape, translating skills into compelling success stories, personalising your narrative, and staying true to yourself. With these strategies in your playbook, you are well on your way to creating a resume that doesn't just open doors but ensures you're remembered long after they've been closed. From paper to person, let your journey begin.

A. Understanding the Purpose of a Resume

Before we delve into the specifics of crafting an AI/ML PM resume, it's crucial to understand the primary purpose of a resume. A resume is not just a document listing your job experiences and education; it's a strategic tool designed to capture the attention of hiring managers, demonstrate your suitability for the role, and convince them to invite you for an interview.

Remember, hiring managers often review dozens, if not hundreds, of resumes for a single job opening. Therefore, your resume should be concise, clear, and compelling. It should highlight your most relevant skills and experiences and demonstrate how these align with the role you're applying for.

B. Resume Structure

A well-structured resume makes it easy for hiring managers to quickly find the information they're looking for. Generally, a resume should include the following sections:

Contact Information: This includes your full name, phone number, email address, and LinkedIn profile link. Ensure that your email address is professional and that your LinkedIn profile is updated and complements your resume.

Objective or Summary: A brief statement at the beginning of your resume that outlines your career goals and why you're applying for the job. This is an excellent place to highlight how your skills and experiences make you a great fit for an AI/ML PM role.

Experience: This section should detail your professional experiences, with a focus on roles and responsibilities relevant to AI/ML PM. Start with your most recent job and work your way back. For each position, list your job title, the name of the organisation, dates of employment, and key responsibilities and achievements.

Education: List your highest degree first, followed by any other relevant qualifications. Be sure to include the name of the institution, the degree earned, and the date of graduation. If you've completed any relevant coursework or projects, it might be beneficial to mention them here.

Skills: This section should highlight the skills you possess that are relevant to an AI/ML PM role. This could include both technical skills, such as proficiency in specific AI/ML tools and algorithms, and soft skills like leadership and communication.

Certifications and Publications: If you've earned any certifications or published any research or articles relevant to AI/ML, be sure to include them. This can demonstrate your commitment to the field and your expertise.

C. Tailoring Your Resume

When it comes to crafting an impactful resume, one size doesn't fit all. It's important to tailor your resume to each specific job application. This means carefully reading the job description to understand what the employer is looking for and then highlighting the skills, experiences, and achievements that align with these requirements.

For an AI/ML PM role, this might involve highlighting your experiences with AI/ML projects, showcasing your ability to bridge the gap between technical teams and other stakeholders, or demonstrating your understanding of the AI/ML product lifecycle.

D. Quantifying Achievements

One effective way to make your resume stand out is to quantify your achievements. Instead of merely stating your responsibilities, try to provide specific examples of your impact and quantify them where possible.

For instance, instead of saying, "Managed an AI project", you might say, "Led a team of 5 engineers in the successful completion of an AI project, which improved the company's predictive analysis accuracy by 20%." This not only makes your achievements more tangible but also demonstrates the direct value you've brought to your past roles.

E. Emphasising Relevant Skills and Experiences

As an AI/ML PM, you'll need a blend of technical, business, and interpersonal skills. Your resume should reflect this.

For example, you might highlight your technical skills by detailing your experience with specific AI/ML technologies or your understanding of the AI/ML development process. On the business side, you might focus on your strategic thinking skills or your ability to understand and translate business needs into technical requirements. For interpersonal skills, you might discuss your experience in leading teams, working with diverse stakeholders, or managing conflict.

If you're transitioning from a different field, remember that many skills are transferable. For instance, your experience in project management, data analysis, or stakeholder management can be valuable in an AI/ML PM role. Be sure to highlight these on your resume.

F. Avoiding Common Mistakes

Mistakes on your resume can leave a poor first impression. Some common mistakes to avoid include typos and grammatical errors, inconsistent formatting, too much jargon, and including irrelevant information. Be sure to thoroughly proofread your resume, and consider having a trusted friend or mentor review it as well.

G. Leveraging Resume Resources

There are many resources available to help you create a standout resume. This includes online resume templates, resume writing services, and career guidance from mentors or career centres. Leveraging these resources can help you create a polished and professional resume.

H. Continuously Updating Your Resume

Your resume should be a living document that you continually update as you gain new skills, experiences, and achievements. Even if you're not actively job searching, regularly updating your resume ensures you're always ready to seize new opportunities when they arise.

Closing Thoughts

Crafting an impactful AI/ML PM resume takes time and thought, but the effort can pay off in the form of job interviews and, ultimately, job offers. By understanding the purpose of a resume, structuring it effectively, tailoring it to each job application, quantifying your achievements, emphasising your relevant skills and experiences, avoiding common mistakes, leveraging resume resources, and continuously updating your resume, you'll be well on your way to creating a resume that opens doors to exciting AI/ML PM opportunities.

In the following chapter, we'll examine the role of effective networking strategies in preparing for your AI/ML PM interview. After all, sometimes, it's not just about what you know but who you know.

Chapter 6

Writing a Convincing Cover Letter

A cover letter is a powerful tool, though often underrated, that accompanies your resume, playing a central role in narrating your professional journey. It's your stage to tell your story, depict your passion for the role, and showcase how your unique blend of skills and experiences aligns with the AI/ML product management role you're pursuing. In this chapter, we explore the craft of writing a convincing cover letter that leaves a lasting first impression on your potential employer.

Setting the Scene: The Importance of a Cover Letter

In the competitive landscape of the AI/ML product management job market, setting yourself apart is paramount. A cover letter gives you the chance to do just that. Unlike the resume, which lays out your qualifications and experience in a structured format, the cover letter is a more personal, narrative-driven document. It is a window into your professional soul, offering insights into your character, ambition, and the unique value you can bring to the role.

Understanding the Anatomy of a Cover Letter

A convincing cover letter is more than a summary of your resume. It should be structured, concise, and written with a clear purpose in mind. The typical cover letter consists of an introduction where you express your interest in the role, a body where you delve into your experiences and skills, and a conclusion where you reiterate your enthusiasm and propose the next steps.

Crafting Your Narrative: Show, Don't Tell

The secret to a compelling cover letter lies in your ability to show rather than tell. Instead of stating that you are "a problem solver," narrate an instance where your problem-solving skills made a significant difference. By turning your skills and experiences into engaging narratives, you offer a glimpse of how you operate in real-world situations, thereby instilling a sense of confidence in your potential employer.

Creating Connection: The Power of Personalisation

Personalisation forms the heart of a compelling cover letter. It's essential to show that you have taken the time to understand the company, its values, and how the role you're applying for fits into the larger picture. Make explicit connections between your experiences and the job requirements. Remember, your goal is to depict a clear image of why you are not just a good but the perfect candidate for the job.

The Art of Authenticity

While it's essential to put your best foot forward, it's equally important to be authentic. Use your genuine voice and avoid jargon or buzzwords. Authenticity resonates, creating a connection that can't be forged otherwise.

In summary, writing a convincing cover letter is an art that combines understanding the structure, crafting engaging narratives, personalising your story to align with the job role, and being authentic. By mastering this craft, your cover letter will cease to be just an accessory to your resume but a powerful testament to your candidacy for the AI/ML product management role. It's time to pick up the pen and start crafting your narrative.

A. The Purpose of a Cover Letter

Before we begin, it's essential to understand what a cover letter is and its purpose. Contrary to popular belief, a cover letter isn't a mere repetition of your resume. Instead, it's an opportunity to provide context for your resume, delve into experiences that highlight your qualifications, express your passion for the job and the company, and give a glimpse of your personality.

A well-crafted cover letter can make a significant difference, especially in a competitive field like AI/ML product management. A successful cover letter paints a vivid picture of your professional narrative and why you're interested in and qualified for this particular role.

B. Structure of a Cover Letter

A convincing cover letter usually consists of the following elements:

Header and Salutation: Like any formal letter, begin with your contact information, the date, and the hiring manager's contact information. If you're unsure of the hiring manager's name, "Dear Hiring Manager" or "Dear [Company Name] Team" is acceptable.

Introduction: Start by introducing yourself and stating the role you're applying for. You can also include where or how you found the job listing. This section is crucial as it sets the tone for the rest of the letter.

Body: The body of your cover letter should include one or two paragraphs detailing why you're a good fit for the role. Discuss relevant experiences, skills, and achievements and how they align with the job requirements. This is your chance to showcase your understanding of AI/ML and your capabilities as a PM.

Company-Specific Paragraph: It's beneficial to include a paragraph that shows you've done your research about the company. Demonstrate enthusiasm for the company's mission, values, or projects and explain why they resonate with you. Also, articulate how you could contribute to the company's goals.

Conclusion: In the concluding paragraph, summarise your qualifications, restate your interest in the role, and thank the hiring manager for their time. Also, mention your availability for an interview and your eagerness to discuss your candidacy further.

Formal Closing: Close the letter formally with phrases like "Best regards," "Sincerely," or "Yours faithfully," followed by your name and signature.

C. Tailoring Your Cover Letter

The cover letter stands as a testament to your professional journey, highlighting your commitment and interest in the role you're applying for. Just as your bespoke suit, tailored to your unique measurements, conveys a sartorial elegance and personal style, so too must your cover letter be precisely fitted to each AI/ML product management job application.

Generic, one-size-fits-all cover letters are easily spotted, projecting a lack of effort and authenticity, and can severely impact your chances of landing the role. In this chapter, we explore how to skillfully tailor your cover letter, aligning it with the job's specific requirements to demonstrate your attention to detail and sincere interest in the role.

The Blueprint: Understanding the Job Description

The first step towards tailoring your cover letter is carefully dissecting the job description. This document serves as the blueprint for the position, providing insights into the role's key responsibilities, required skills and qualifications, and the company's expectations from the prospective candidate. Treat the job description as a map guiding you to highlight the relevant aspects of your professional journey.

Creating Alignment: Matching Skills and Experiences

Having dissected the job description, you now need to match your skills and experiences with the role's requirements. Each skill or experience you mention should echo a requirement listed in the job description. Be wary of generic terms; instead, replace them with specific examples demonstrating how you've applied these skills in real-world scenarios.

Personalisation: The Essential Ingredient

Tailoring your cover letter extends beyond mere skill alignment. The essence of personalisation lies in connecting with the company's ethos and understanding its unique challenges and aspirations. Research the company extensively and weave your findings into your cover letter, indicating why you are genuinely attracted to the organisation and how you envision contributing to its growth.

Telling Your Story: Relevance and Resonance

Your cover letter is your professional narrative. When tailoring your cover letter, ensure that each paragraph, sentence, even word, contributes to the story you're trying to tell. Remember, relevance is key. Each aspect of your story should resonate with the job you're applying for and add weight to your candidacy.

Ending on a High Note: A Call to Action

An often-overlooked aspect of tailoring your cover letter is how you conclude it. End on a high note, reiterating your interest in the role and the unique value you bring. Propose the next steps, perhaps suggesting a meeting or call to discuss your application further.

In conclusion, tailoring your cover letter is an art that requires understanding the job description, aligning your skills and experiences, personalising your approach, weaving a relevant narrative, and ending with a confident call to action. By mastering this art, you can ensure your cover letter makes an indelible impression, compelling the hiring manager to explore your candidacy further.

D. Focusing on the Employer's Needs

One of the most prevalent pitfalls in drafting cover letters is an overemphasis on the job applicant's aspirations, with scant regard for the employer's needs. While it's crucial to elucidate how the role aligns with your career trajectory, the primary focus should pivot on how your repertoire of skills and experiences could be a boon to the prospective employer. This chapter peels back the layers of the 'employer-centric approach' to cover letter composition, providing you with an enlightened perspective to cast yourself as the solution to the employer's needs.

The Cardinal Rule: Understanding the Employer
Employer-centricity in your cover letter begins with a comprehensive understanding of the employer. Get under the skin of the organisation – understand its mission, values, challenges, and goals. By threading this understanding through your cover letter, you communicate that your focus is not merely on landing the job but on contributing to the organisation's objectives.

The Value Proposition: Your Unique Offering
Position yourself as a value proposition. Rather than merely stating your skills and experiences, delve into the tangible benefits that these could bring to the employer. This might involve driving efficiency, solving specific problems, bringing fresh perspectives, or contributing to innovation. Employers aren't just looking for candidates with the right skills – they're looking for candidates who can apply these skills to deliver results.

Answering the Call: Responding to Job Requirements
A central part of focusing on the employer's needs involves explicitly responding to the job requirements listed in the job description. For each requirement, detail your relevant skills or experiences and how they will enable you to fulfil that requirement. By doing this, you communicate that you

understand the employer's needs and are equipped to meet them.

The Art of Empathy: Aligning with the Company Culture

Focusing on the employer's needs isn't just about meeting job requirements – it's also about aligning with the company's culture. Demonstrate your understanding and alignment with the company culture, showing that you will not only fit in but will also contribute to the ethos that the company upholds.

The Parting Shot: Reinforcing Your Suitability

In your concluding paragraph, reiterate your understanding of the employer's needs and reinforce how you are uniquely positioned to meet these needs. This leaves the employer with a lasting impression of you as a candidate who has their needs at the forefront and is ready to contribute to their goals.

By placing the employer's needs centre-stage in your cover letter, you demonstrate a deep understanding of the role and the value you bring. This approach helps you stand out from the sea of applicants who focus solely on their needs and ambitions. Remember, the essence of a cover letter lies in its ability to communicate that you are not just a great candidate but the right candidate to fill the void in their organisation.

E. Showcasing Your Communication Skills

Your cover letter acts as a mirror, reflecting your aptitude for written communication—a critical facet of a Product Manager's role. In a realm where communication bridges the gap between technical and non-technical stakeholders, your ability to convey your thoughts in a lucid and compelling manner is vital. This chapter decodes the art of encapsulating your skills and experiences in a succinct, grammatically flawless cover letter that resonates with prospective employers.

Language and Syntax: The Fine Art of Clarity

Before we delve into the finer points of demonstrating your skills and experience, it is paramount to focus on the fundamentals. Your cover letter should be free from syntactical errors, demonstrating a command of language that communicates your thoughts effectively. It isn't about crafting verbose sentences but rather using the right words in the right place.

Structure and Flow: The Architectonics of Your Letter

The way you structure your cover letter is just as important as its content. A logically structured cover letter tells the reader that you think systematically—a crucial skill for a PM. Start with a brief introduction about yourself and the role you're applying for, follow this with the body detailing your skills and experiences, and finally, conclude by reaffirming your suitability for the role and expressing enthusiasm for potential next steps.

Formatting: A Professional First Impression

Proper formatting is often overlooked but is essential for demonstrating your professionalism. This involves aligning your text, keeping consistent margins, using appropriate spacing, and utilising bullet points for ease of reading where necessary. Your cover letter's presentation reflects your attention to detail—and attribute every employer appreciates.

Purposeful Brevity: Be Concise, Yet Compelling

With employers often sifting through stacks of applications, your cover letter should be as concise as possible without sacrificing the quality of your message. Every sentence should serve a clear purpose—explaining why you're applying, why you're a good fit, and how you could add value to the company.

Authenticity: Speak with Your Own Voice

Remember, your cover letter is a reflection of you. Don't be afraid to let your personality shine through in your writing. Authenticity creates a connection with the reader and helps you stand out from the sea of boilerplate letters.

In essence, showcasing your communication skills in your cover letter involves more than just avoiding grammatical errors. It's about clarity of message, logical structure, professional formatting, purposeful brevity, and a touch of your unique personality. The pen may be mightier than the sword, but it's the skilled hand that wields it that makes the real impact. Make sure your cover letter, a silent ambassador of your communication skills, makes the right impact.

F. Utilising Action Verbs and Quantifying Achievements

The strength of your cover letter can often hinge upon your choice of words. The right verbiage can vividly depict your capabilities, adding a dynamic edge to your application. This chapter delves into two pivotal elements of a persuasive cover letter: the use of action verbs and the quantification of your achievements. By applying these techniques, your cover letter can become a compelling showcase of your talents, transforming abstract competencies into palpable achievements.

Action Speaks: The Impact of Action Verbs

The choice of verbs in your cover letter can be the difference between a passive list of responsibilities and an engaging depiction of your capabilities. Action verbs such as 'managed', 'led', 'designed', 'implemented', 'analysed', and others, give your letter a sense of movement and progress. They transform mundane tasks into proactive initiatives, showcasing your abilities to take charge, drive results, and make an impact.

For example, instead of saying "I was assigned to oversee a team of data scientists," using an action verb transforms this into "I adeptly managed a team of data scientists."

The Numbers Game: Quantifying Achievements

Beyond descriptive language, your cover letter will also benefit immensely from quantified achievements. Including specific figures and percentages lends credibility and adds a tangible dimension to your accomplishments. Quantification provides an objective perspective on your potential as a future AI/ML product manager, depicting a clear picture of your capabilities.

Consider the following example: rather than stating, "I significantly improved the predictive accuracy of our AI model," a quantified statement would read, "I spearheaded an initiative to refine our AI model, resulting in a 25% improvement in predictive accuracy."

Action Verbs and Quantification: The Perfect Harmony

Combining action verbs with quantified achievements in your cover letter offers the best of both worlds. It illustrates your dynamic approach to work and provides measurable evidence of your successes.

For instance, instead of writing, "I was responsible for leading a project for developing an AI model," a more impactful statement could read, "I successfully led a team of 5 data scientists and engineers to develop an AI model, culminating in a 25% improvement in predictive accuracy."

When harnessed correctly, the potency of action verbs and quantified achievements can revolutionise your cover letter. They transform it from a passive summary into a powerful testament to your ability to make a significant contribution as an AI/ML product manager.

G. Avoiding Common Mistakes

The path to a compelling cover letter is fraught with pitfalls. It is a fine line between asserting your potential as an AI/ML product manager and rambling redundantly. Striking the perfect balance requires understanding the common mistakes candidates often make when writing their cover letters. This chapter aims to guide you around these pitfalls, helping you craft a cover letter that strikes a chord without hitting a wrong note.

The Sin of Verbosity: Length Does Matter

More is not always better, and in the context of cover letters, brevity, indeed is the soul of wit. Recruiters often have to sift through hundreds of applications, so your cover letter must make its impact succinctly. A single page is typically sufficient to capture your suitability for the role without exhausting the reader's patience.

Echolalia: Avoiding Repetition of Your CV

Your cover letter and CV are separate documents for a reason. While your CV outlines your skills, qualifications, and career trajectory, your cover letter adds colour to this black-and-white outline by weaving these elements into a coherent narrative. Simply repeating your CV verbatim in your cover letter is a wasted opportunity to build a deeper connection with the hiring manager.

Informality and Over-Personalisation: Striking the Right Tone

While authenticity is desirable, there is a fine line between personable and overly personal. Strive for a professional tone and avoid sharing excessively personal anecdotes or informal language. Remember, your cover letter is your chance to demonstrate your suitability for the role, not your aptitude for small talk.

Meticulousness: The Devil is in the Details

In the world of AI/ML product management, attention to detail is a prized asset. Typos, grammatical errors, or incorrect company names not only reflect poorly on your written communication skills but they also raise questions about your attention to detail. Proofreading your letter multiple times or even getting a second pair of eyes can help you avoid these pitfalls.

Mind the Gap: Addressing Career Gaps

If your career history has gaps, your cover letter is an ideal place to address them. Be honest and straightforward, focusing on what you did during that time that is relevant to the role you're applying for.

Writing a cover letter is much like navigating a minefield, with the potential for seemingly minor missteps to trigger major setbacks.

However, with careful attention to these common mistakes, you can ensure your cover letter propels you towards securing that coveted AI/ML product manager interview.

H. Seeking Feedback

Embarking upon the journey of job applications can be akin to venturing into uncharted territory. Having a guiding light in the form of feedback can be instrumental in navigating these waters successfully. This chapter emphasises the significance of seeking feedback on your cover letter, a document that could be your golden ticket to securing your desired AI/ML Product Manager role.

The Importance of a Fresh Pair of Eyes

Crafting your cover letter can often be a deeply personal endeavour, requiring introspection and a detailed recounting of your professional journey. While your intimate knowledge of your career trajectory is an asset, it can also sometimes become a limitation. It might make you oblivious to gaps in your narrative, oversights in detail, or assumptions about industry knowledge.

Inviting a mentor, career coach, or a trusted colleague to review your cover letter can bring a fresh perspective to the table. Their external viewpoint can help spot these pitfalls, ensure clarity in communication, and refine the letter to resonate with your potential employer.

Feedback: An Exercise in Humility and Growth

Seeking feedback requires humility and an openness to critique - qualities that are highly regarded in the field of AI/ML product management. This process of seeking advice and guidance reveals your willingness to learn and grow, mirroring the iterative process inherent to AI/ML projects. The feedback loop, so central to improving AI/ML models, finds a parallel in your journey as a product manager. It enables you to continually refine your approach, enhancing the strength of your application with each iteration.

Turning Feedback into Action

Feedback, however, is only as valuable as what you do with it. When you receive critiques, take them into careful consideration and apply them constructively to improve your cover letter. The purpose isn't to have your letter written by someone else but to gain insights that you might not have considered.

For instance, you might discover that while you thought you were effectively highlighting your achievements, an outside perspective might indicate that you are underselling your accomplishments. Conversely, what you perceive as demonstrating enthusiasm, a reviewer might interpret as overzealousness.

Navigating Forward with Feedback

In conclusion, feedback is an essential component in the crafting of an effective cover letter. It fosters growth, encourages improvement, and is a testament to your commitment to landing your dream AI/ML Product Manager role. By acknowledging that 'no man is an island', and embracing a collaborative approach to your job applications, you will be one step closer to going from zero to offer.

I. Following Up

In the grand scheme of job applications, many overlook one vital component that, when executed thoughtfully, can reinforce your earnestness and initiative: the follow-up. This chapter aims to elucidate the delicate dance of following up on your AI/ML product management application, setting you apart from other candidates in a tasteful, professional manner.

Understanding the Value of a Follow-Up

In the pursuit of your dream role, each step carries importance, from crafting an impactful resume to tailoring a compelling cover letter. Yet, the journey doesn't end at submission. A well-timed, respectful follow-up can provide a subtle reminder of your interest and eagerness to the hiring manager, ensuring your application stays fresh in their mind amid the deluge of candidates.

The Delicate Art of Timing

Timing is an integral aspect of following up. It's important to wait long enough to give the hiring team time to review applications. An ideal window for follow-up is generally a week or two posts the application deadline. Sending a follow-up too soon can come off as pushy or desperate, while waiting too long might risk your application being forgotten.

Respecting Boundaries

Whilst the follow-up indicates your continued interest, it's crucial to maintain respect for the hiring manager's process. They likely have a multitude of applications to review, a task requiring careful consideration and time. A constant barrage of follow-ups can be counterproductive, creating an impression of impatience rather than initiative.

Crafting the Follow-Up

Your follow-up communication, like your cover letter, is an extension of your professional persona. It should be succinct and polite and express your ongoing interest in the role. Reiterate your enthusiasm, but avoid repeating the contents of your cover letter or resume. Instead, take this opportunity to thank them for considering your application and express your readiness for the next steps.

Navigating Unresponsive Waters

In some instances, you may not receive a response to your follow-up. In such cases, it's essential to remain professional and composed. Employers' silence shouldn't be taken as a negative reflection of your capabilities. Numerous factors might contribute to the lack of a response, including internal processes or the sheer volume of applications.

If you face this scenario, it's advisable to move forward and focus on other opportunities. Remember, in the realm of job applications, perseverance is key.

Conclusion

Crafting a compelling cover letter is an art that can significantly increase your chances of landing an AI/ML PM job. By understanding its purpose, structuring it effectively, tailoring it to each job application, focusing on the employer's needs, showcasing your communication skills, utilising action verbs, quantifying achievements, avoiding common mistakes, seeking feedback, and following up appropriately, you'll be well-positioned to grab the hiring manager's attention.

In the next chapter, we'll discuss the importance of company research in preparing for your AI/ML PM interview and how it can set you apart from other candidates.

Chapter 7

Conducting In-depth Company Research

In the competitive landscape of AI/ML product management, standing out from the crowd often requires more than a stellar CV or a compelling cover letter. It necessitates a level of commitment and dedication that extends beyond the traditional bounds of job seeking. This is where conducting in-depth company research comes to the fore. This chapter aims to guide you through this process, demonstrating how it can enrich your understanding, boost your confidence, and ultimately increase your chances of landing the desired role.

Why In-Depth Company Research Matters

At first glance, extensive company research might seem like an arduous task. However, the insights gleaned can have far-reaching impacts. Understanding a company's mission, vision, values, products or services, market position, culture, and current affairs allows you to assess whether the company aligns with your career aspirations.

Moreover, being well-versed about the company indicates to potential employers that you are genuinely interested in the role and are proactive enough to delve beyond the surface. It can help shape your responses during the interview, allowing you to align your answers with the company's needs and culture.

A. The Value of Company Research

The significance of conducting comprehensive research about a potential employer can never be overstated. A profound understanding of the company allows you to tailor your application and interview responses to suit the organisation's needs. This not only aids you in demonstrating your alignment with the company's goals but also positions you as a proactive and motivated candidate.

B. Understanding the Company's AI/ML Products or Services

Start by exploring the company's existing AI/ML products or services. Understand how these offerings function and how they add value to the company and its customers. Pay attention to details such as the technologies they utilise, the problems they solve, and their unique selling propositions. For tech giants, it's important to identify the specific team or product you're applying to and focus your research accordingly.

C. Examining the Company's Business Model

Next, familiarise yourself with the company's business model. How does it generate revenue? Who are its key customers? What market segments does it operate in? Gaining a deep understanding of how the business works will enable you to speak knowledgeably about the company's strategic goals during your interviews.

D. Exploring the Company's Culture and Values

Understanding the company's culture and values can give you insights into what it's like to work there. Do they value innovation and creativity or prioritise structure and processes? What is their stance on diversity and inclusion? How do they support employee well-being and growth? Familiarity with the company's culture can help you gauge whether it's a good fit for you and how to present yourself as a suitable candidate.

E. Identifying the Company's Market Position

Investigate the company's standing in the market and its competitive landscape. Who are its primary competitors, and how do its products or services compare to those of its rivals? Understanding the company's market position can provide a context for its strategic priorities and allow you to articulate how you can contribute to its competitive advantage.

F. Staying Current with the Company's News and Developments

It's critical to stay up-to-date with the company's recent news and developments. Have they launched any new AI/ML products or features? Have they entered new markets or partnerships? Were they part of any controversies? Following the company's news can indicate your interest in and dedication to the role.

G. Utilising Various Information Sources

There are various sources of information you can use for your research, including:

Company's Website: This is usually the best starting point for your research. The 'About Us', 'Our Products/Services', 'Newsroom', or 'Blog' sections can provide valuable insights.

Social Media and Professional Networking Platforms:
The company's LinkedIn, Twitter, Facebook, and other
social media platforms can offer up-to-date news and help
you understand its culture and values.

Employee Reviews: Websites such as Glassdoor can
provide insights into the company's work environment and
employee experiences.

Financial Reports and Industry Analysis: If the company
is publicly traded, you can find valuable information in its
annual reports and financial statements. Industry analysis
reports, available through platforms like Gartner and
Forrester, can also be beneficial.

H. Preparing for Interview Questions

Armed with this knowledge, you can now anticipate and
prepare for potential interview questions. How would you
improve a specific AI/ML product or feature the company
offers? How do you see the company's market position
evolving in the coming years, and how would you
contribute to this? You'll also be better equipped to ask
thoughtful questions about the company, showing your
depth of understanding and enthusiasm.

I. Tailoring Your Application

Use your research findings to tailor your resume and cover
letter. Highlight relevant experiences and skills that align
with the company's needs and aspirations. Show how your
values align with the company's culture and mission. This
approach shows that you've taken the time to understand
the company and see yourself as part of it.

J. Adapting Your Communication Style

Understanding the company's culture can also provide insights into its preferred communication style. Is it formal or casual? Does it value brevity or detail? Adapting your communication style to match the company's can create a positive impression and show your cultural fit.

K. Demonstrating Your Knowledge During the Interview

During the interview, demonstrate your knowledge about the company, its AI/ML products or services, its market position, and recent news or developments. This can set you apart from other candidates and show your genuine interest in the role.

L. Preparing for Potential Changes

Remember that companies, especially in the fast-paced field of AI/ML, are constantly evolving. Keep abreast of any changes in the company's strategies, products or services, and market position as your application process progresses. This readiness to adapt will further exemplify your commitment and adaptability.

M. Respecting Confidentiality

While conducting your research, you might come across sensitive or confidential information, especially if you have connections within the company. Always respect this confidentiality. Use only publicly available information in your application and interviews, and never give the impression that you have access to insider information.

Conclusion

In-depth company research is a powerful tool in your AI/ML PM job application journey. It allows you to tailor your application and interviews to the company's needs, showcase your initiative and interest, ask insightful questions, and demonstrate your potential as a valuable addition to the company. As you prepare for your interview, remember this: the more you know about the company, the better prepared you'll be to present yourself as the ideal candidate.

In the following chapters, we'll delve into the various stages of the AI/ML PM interview process and offer practical strategies to help you excel at each one. As the Chinese proverb goes, "The work well begun is the work half done." So let's start this journey towards your dream job on a strong note!

Part III

The AI/ML PM Interview Process

The AI and ML Product Manager interview process is unique. It melds the complexity of technology with the abstract art of human management, and the scrutiny of the interview process mirrors this challenging balance. In this section of the book, we will journey through this intricate labyrinth, shedding light on its twists and turns while equipping you with a compass that enables you to navigate it confidently.

The AI/ML PM interview process typically comprises five key stages:
- The screening interview
- The technical interview
- The behavioural interview
- The case study interview
- The on-site interview

This might sound intimidating, but think of it as a series of conversations, each a chance to show why you are the right person for the role. It's a chance to tell your story.

Screening Interview

This first interview is often conducted by a recruiter. It's the first 'gate' of the process, where you'll discuss your background, your interest in the role, and the company. While this stage may seem relatively casual, it's crucial to prepare for it as seriously as you would for any other step. First impressions are lasting, and the screening interview is where you make that initial impression.

Technical Interview

Next comes the technical interview. This stage is designed to assess your understanding of AI/ML and your problem-solving skills. The questions will likely relate to your knowledge of machine learning algorithms, data structures, and relevant technologies. Be prepared to discuss recent AI/ML advancements, and don't be surprised if you're asked to solve a problem on a whiteboard. The aim here is to see not just if you know your stuff but also how you think.

Behavioural Interview

The behavioural interview is where the interviewer tries to understand you as a person and as a potential colleague. They want to gauge if you are someone who would fit into their team culture and work environment. Expect questions about your past experiences, especially situations where you dealt with conflict, managed stress, or demonstrated leadership. Be prepared to showcase your soft skills and use the STAR method (Situation, Task, Action, Result) to structure your responses.

Case Study Interview

The case study interview is unique to the product management role. In this stage, you will be presented with a hypothetical product scenario and asked to devise a solution. The interviewer will be looking at your strategic thinking, your ability to handle ambiguity, and your decision-making process. It's also a chance to show your understanding of AI/ML and how it can be leveraged to solve real-world problems.

On-site Interview

Finally, the on-site interview. This is the culmination of the interview process, where you meet the team, possibly the executives, and have a series of interviews. These sessions may be a mix of technical, behavioural, and case study discussions. It's the last leg of the journey and the step that could lead to the job offer.

To sum up, the AI/ML PM interview process is rigorous and multi-faceted, designed to assess a range of skills and traits. But remember, it's not a one-way street. It's also your opportunity to determine if the company is the right fit for you, your goals, and your career aspirations. As we navigate through each of these stages in detail in the chapters that follow, you'll gain a deep understanding of the process and be well-prepared to tackle each stage with confidence and finesse. Ultimately, the goal of this journey is not just to get a job offer but to find a role where you can thrive, contribute, and grow.

The complexity of the AI/ML PM role means that your potential employer will want to evaluate you from a variety of angles, and they will do this using several interviewing techniques. Some companies might add or subtract stages or blend them together, but the five core stages mentioned are present in most processes.

Let's delve a little deeper into each stage to fully understand their purpose and how you can best prepare for them.

Screening Interview:

In this stage, it's essential to convey your enthusiasm and understanding of the role. Often, recruiters aren't deeply technical, so keep your language understandable for a broad audience. Highlight your relevant experience and explain why you're interested in AI/ML product management specifically and this role in particular. Be prepared to explain career transitions, projects, and other highlights from your CV.

Technical Interview:

Don't panic at the phrase 'technical interview'. You're not expected to write complex code or build an AI model. Instead, this stage assesses your understanding of AI/ML concepts, the technical context surrounding them, and your ability to apply this knowledge to real-world scenarios.

Review your AI/ML fundamentals, have a few examples ready from your experience where you applied these, and be ready to discuss recent developments in the field.

Behavioural Interview:

During this stage, it's vital to communicate that you're not just technically proficient but also a collaborative, communicative, and dedicated team player. Be prepared to tell stories that demonstrate your skills. And remember, the goal here is not just to tell what you did but to convey how you think and work.

Case Study Interview:

This is where you show your problem-solving skills in action. You'll have to address a hypothetical situation involving an AI/ML product and provide a solution. Your answer should demonstrate a clear understanding of the problem, a logical approach to solving it, and a comprehensive solution that includes a discussion of potential challenges and how to address them.

On-site Interview:

This is the final step and often the most comprehensive one. You're likely to meet a variety of people from different roles, and each one will be looking to understand a different aspect of your fit for the role. It's a long day but remember: You've made it this far because they're seriously considering you for the role.

All these stages might seem overwhelming, but each one is just a piece of the puzzle. Together, they create a holistic view of your capabilities as a potential AI/ML Product Manager. Navigating them successfully requires understanding their purpose, preparing accordingly, and then being yourself during the process. You have a unique set of experiences, skills, and ideas - these are what companies want to see.

In the following chapters, we will break down each of these stages, offering practical advice on how to excel in them.

From common questions to effective strategies, we'll arm you with all the knowledge and tools you need to give a stellar performance at every stage of the interview process. This journey might be challenging, but with preparation and the right mindset, it's one that can lead you to an exciting career in AI/ML Product Management. So, let's dive in and start preparing for your successful journey from zero to offer.

Chapter 8
Effective Networking Strategies

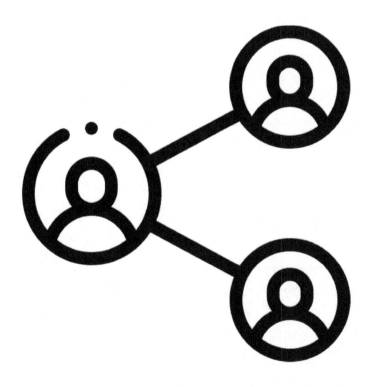

Welcome to the world of professional networking. The power of a well-developed network can be quite transformational in one's journey to becoming an accomplished AI/ML Product Manager. The process of networking, despite its daunting reputation, is merely about creating and nurturing relationships within your industry, expanding your knowledge, and uncovering new opportunities. This chapter is crafted to provide you with strategic insights and techniques that will propel your networking journey within the AI/ML Product Management field.

A. Understanding Networking

The first step towards effective networking is demystifying what it truly entails. Contrary to popular belief, networking is not a transactional process where one's sole purpose is to gain immediate advantages. Instead, it is a relationship-building exercise, a continuous process that requires patience, effort, and genuine interest in creating meaningful professional connections. Remember, networking is as much about giving as it is about receiving; you'll often find yourself learning from others whilst sharing your knowledge and experiences in the realm of AI/ML product management.

B. The Mindset for Networking

Approach networking with an open mind and a genuine curiosity to learn from others. Engage with people not merely as potential links to job opportunities, but as individuals who can offer fresh perspectives and insights that can broaden your understanding of the field. This mindset can alleviate any apprehension associated with networking and render the experience more enjoyable and productive.

C. Cultivating Your Network

Start networking within your existing circles—colleagues, professors, classmates, and friends in the field—and gradually extend your reach. Attend industry-specific events, join relevant online communities, and contribute to forums or discussions related to AI/ML product management. Make sure to interact with professionals across various roles and levels in AI/ML Product Management to gain diverse insights into the industry.

D. Informational Interviews

One of the most effective networking tools at your disposal is informational interviews. These are informal conversations with professionals who hold positions or work in companies that interest you. Reach out to individuals in your network or use platforms like LinkedIn to connect with potential interviewees. Approach them with a clear request for advice, not employment, and engage them with thoughtful questions about their roles, career paths, and experiences in the field.

E. Building Your Personal Brand

Creating a robust personal brand can propel your networking efforts by making you memorable and demonstrating your passion and knowledge in AI/ML product management. A strong personal brand—displayed through your online presence, industry engagements, and even informal conversations—can draw people towards you, enhancing your networking effectiveness. Be sure to communicate your values, aspirations, and unique selling proposition consistently across all professional touchpoints.

F. Networking Etiquette
While networking, remember to respect the other person's time and keep your interactions professional. Aim for genuine, meaningful conversations rather than surface-level exchanges. Show gratitude when others help you and look for ways to reciprocate.

G. Leveraging Your Network
Your network can become a goldmine of opportunities when you're ready to take the plunge into the AI/ML PM job market. Share your career aspirations and target companies with your network. Someone in your network might work for a company you're interested in, and their referral could significantly improve your chances of landing an interview.

H. Nurturing Your Network
Networking is a continuous endeavour. Even after landing your dream role, stay in touch with your network. Share interesting articles, congratulate them on professional accomplishments, and support them when needed.

I. Networking In The Digital Age
In today's interconnected world, networking extends beyond face-to-face interactions. Digital platforms like LinkedIn, Twitter, and niche industry forums offer numerous opportunities to connect with professionals globally. Regularly sharing and engaging with AI/ML content on these platforms can showcase your industry knowledge and attract like-minded professionals.

However, while networking online, remember to maintain professionalism and respect. Do not send mass connection requests or generic messages. Personalise your communication and ensure your interaction adds value to the recipient. Regularly update your profile to reflect your current skills, experiences, and interests.

J. Networking At Events And Conferences
Industry-specific events and conferences are networking goldmines. You can meet and learn from industry leaders, share ideas with peers, and even catch the attention of potential employers. To make the most of these events, research the attendees and prepare relevant questions or conversation starters. Engage deeply in conversations, and focus on the quality of interactions rather than quantity.

K. Creating A Networking Plan
Having a strategic plan can maximise your networking effectiveness. Identify the types of professionals you want to connect with and the knowledge you hope to gain. Prioritise your networking efforts accordingly. Also, set realistic goals for your networking activities, like attending a certain number of industry events or conducting a specific number of
informational interviews.

L. Nurturing Your Connections
Building a connection is just the beginning; the key to a strong network is nurturing these relationships. Stay in touch with your connections through regular, meaningful

interactions. Celebrate their professional accomplishments, share relevant resources, and offer your help when needed. Show genuine interest in their work and express gratitude when they offer you assistance or advice.

M. Building A Supportive Network

Your network should not just be a means to an end but a supportive community that aids in your professional growth. Connect with professionals who inspire you, share your values, and are willing to share their experiences and insights. Seek mentors who can guide you, peers who can relate to your experiences, and mentees to whom you can offer guidance.

N. Leveraging Your Network During Job Search

Your network can be instrumental in your job search process. Sharing your job search goals with your network can lead to job opportunities, referrals, and valuable advice. If someone from your network works at your target company, consider asking them for a referral or insights about the company culture and interview process.

In conclusion, effective networking requires strategy, effort, and authenticity. It's a powerful tool that can boost your career in AI/ML product management by connecting you with opportunities, providing industry insights, and fostering professional growth. The importance of networking cannot be overstated in your journey from zero to offer. It's a testament to the old adage, "It's not just what you know, but who you know." Hence, invest time in nurturing your network and reap the benefits manifold in your AI/ML Product Manager career.

Chapter 9
Decoding The Job Description

Amid the sea of job openings in the vibrant field of AI/ML product management, how do you pinpoint the opportunity that aligns seamlessly with your ambitions and skills? One of the key ways to identify the right fit and strategise your application is by decoding the job description, the roadmap to understanding the employer's needs and expectations. This chapter will serve as your guide to deciphering these crucial documents, positioning you to build compelling applications tailored to each role you target.

What's in a Job Description?

At its core, a job description is a reflection of a company's needs. It outlines the expectations from the potential candidate, the roles and responsibilities they would assume, the skills they must possess, and the kind of experience the company values. Viewing a job description as more than just a list of requirements but as a window into the organisation's culture, priorities, and direction is the first step in decoding it.

Navigating the Structure

Job descriptions typically follow a similar structure: an overview of the role, responsibilities, requirements, preferred skills or qualifications, and details about the company. However, the devil is often in the detail. It's crucial to understand not just what is said but also what is implied, reading between the lines to gain a holistic understanding of the role.

Demystifying the Role Overview

The role overview is an opportunity to comprehend the broad expectations of the job. This includes the objectives of the role, its importance within the company, the team you would be part of, and who you would report to. By understanding the broader context of the role, you can better align your application and interview responses to the key objectives of the job.

Deciphering the Responsibilities

The responsibilities section provides insights into what you will be doing day-to-day. It's key to understand these tasks and how they align with your skills and experiences. Keep in mind that this section often prioritises the most critical tasks at the top. By matching your experiences with these responsibilities, you can demonstrate that you are not just a qualified candidate but the right fit for this specific role.

Interpreting the Requirements

Requirements typically include the mandatory qualifications and skills for the role. They might encompass educational qualifications, years of experience, specific technical skills, or industry knowledge. It's essential to note that meeting every requirement isn't always necessary; a lack of certain skills can be compensated with transferable skills or the potential to learn.

Understanding Preferred Skills or Qualifications

These are not mandatory but could set you apart from other applicants. It's helpful to highlight any that match your profile and consider how you might acquire or demonstrate others. These skills often reflect the company's vision for the role beyond the core requirements, providing a peek into what they value in a candidate.

The Company Overview and Culture

The company details and any mention of culture provide valuable insights into the working environment and the company's values. It's worthwhile to reflect on how these align with your own values and aspirations.

Keywords: The Hidden Language

Particular attention should be paid to recurring themes or keywords in the job description. These reflect the role's core requirements and the company's priorities. Using similar language in your application can create resonance with the hiring team.

Reading Between the Lines

Beyond the explicit information in the job description, there are often hidden insights to be unearthed. The tone and language of the description can hint at the company's culture. The ambitious language might indicate a fast-paced, high-growth environment, while an emphasis on collaboration could suggest a team-oriented culture.

Taking It Forward

Decoding a job description is not a passive reading activity; it's an interactive process. Making notes, highlighting key areas, and jotting down questions that arise will enrich your understanding and give you a head start in preparing for the application and potential interviews.

Researching Beyond the Job Description

While the job description is a crucial resource, further research can supplement your understanding. Company websites, LinkedIn profiles, press releases, and news articles can provide additional context. Conversations with current employees or other professionals in the industry can also yield valuable insights.

Aligning Your Application

Once you've decoded the job description, it's time to align your application. This involves tailoring your CV, cover letter, and any other application materials to reflect the key requirements and priorities highlighted in the job description. For example, if the role heavily emphasises teamwork, be sure to highlight your experience and skills in collaboration.

Preparation for Interview

The job description also serves as a roadmap for interview preparation. You can anticipate questions based on the role's responsibilities and requirements and prepare compelling responses demonstrating your alignment with these areas. Practising responses to potential questions will help you articulate your suitability for the role.

Asking the Right Questions

A final aspect of decoding the job description is identifying areas where you need more information. These queries can be addressed during the interview, demonstrating your thorough understanding of the role and genuine interest in the company.

The Art of Decoding

Decoding a job description is an intriguing blend of artistry and skill, a dance between intuition and reason. To the untrained eye, a job description may appear as merely a list of duties and requirements. However, to the astute job-seeker, it is a coded message, a treasure map pointing towards a wealth of valuable insights.

In this decoding process, intuition serves as your compass, leading you beyond the superficial layers of the text and into the realm of deeper understanding. Your intuition guides you to interpret the subtext, read between the lines, and perceive the subtle nuances that may be missed by others. It enables you to sense the underlying culture of the company, the priorities that may not be explicitly stated, and the vision that the company aspires to realise through the role. Harnessing this intuitive understanding is not an overnight process; it requires a willingness to trust your instincts and an openness to learn from your missteps.

On the other hand, honing your analytical skills equips you with the ability to dissect the job description with surgical precision. This requires practice and perseverance. By analysing numerous job descriptions, you can begin to recognise patterns and familiarise yourself with common industry terms and expectations. The ability to identify the hard skills and experiences required, the soft skills valued, and the performance metrics applied can significantly enhance your preparation efforts.

Additionally, understanding the structure of job descriptions can also streamline the decoding process. Typically, job descriptions include an overview of the company, key responsibilities, qualifications, preferred skills, and, occasionally, details about the work environment and benefits. Navigating this structure becomes smoother with time and practice, enabling you to quickly pinpoint the information you need.

The act of decoding extends further to distinguish between roles that are congruent with your aspirations from those that merely appears to be. It assists you in identifying opportunities that align with your career goals, personal values, and skillset. Not every AI/ML Product Manager role is the same. Different industries, company sizes, and team structures can significantly shape the role and hence, your experience. The ability to discern these differences can be crucial in guiding your job search towards fulfilling and rewarding opportunities.

Why Decoding Matters

Decoding job descriptions does more than just help you understand the role; it helps you understand yourself. It enables you to identify the skills you bring to the table, areas for development, and the type of environment in which you'll thrive. It's a compass guiding you towards roles where you can succeed and be satisfied.

As you journey towards becoming an AI/ML Product Manager, the ability to decode a job description is one of the essential skills you'll need. It's a skill that will guide you in finding the right opportunities, crafting compelling applications, excelling in interviews, and ultimately, landing a role that aligns with your aspirations. So, the next time you're faced with a job description, remember it's more than a list of requirements; it's a code waiting to be cracked.

The game of landing your dream job as an AI/ML Product Manager is no less than a strategic puzzle. Decoding job descriptions form the pieces of this puzzle. With this guide, you're ready to piece together your path from aspirant to offered. As you continue this journey, remember each application is more than a potential job; it's a stepping stone towards your career in AI/ML product management. Make each one count, and you'll be sure to transition from zero to offer.

Chapter 10

The Screening Interview

Embarking on your journey to becoming an AI/ML Product Manager, the first significant landmark you will encounter is the Screening Interview. It is like the gatekeeper guarding the castle of your dreams. However, do not let this analogy intimidate you. Think of it as the initial handshake, a meet-and-greet, with the company. The intent is to make sure you are who you say you are, check your basic qualifications, and ascertain if you might be a good fit for the role.

The screening interview is often conducted by a recruiter or HR personnel, and in some cases, the hiring manager. The interviewer may not possess deep technical knowledge about AI/ML, but they will be adept at evaluating your communication skills, professionalism, and your passion for the role. This chapter aims to equip you with the tools needed to successfully navigate this first crucial stage of your job application journey.

Let's break it down and build our strategy.

Understanding the Screening Interview:

A typical screening interview can range from 15 to 30 minutes, and it's most likely to be conducted over the phone or a video call. Expect questions that allow the interviewer to gain a snapshot of your capabilities and aspirations. Questions may span from your educational background and experience to your understanding of the role, why you are interested in AI/ML product management, and why you are applying to this specific company.

Preparation Is Key:

1. **Master Your CV**: Your curriculum vitae (CV), or resume, is essentially your professional story, concisely scripted and elegantly structured. It is the basis for your initial discussion during the screening interview. It's vital to have an intimate understanding of every element listed on it, as any point may trigger a discussion or query from the interviewer. Can you illustrate how you navigated a particular challenge or led a pivotal project? Are you equipped to articulate how your past roles have nurtured your skills, moulded your perspectives, and contributed to your professional development? Are you ready to discuss career transitions, including the reason you left a previous job or any noticeable gaps in your employment history? Being fluent in your own narrative is key to responding confidently and articulately.

2. **Comprehend the Role**: Being an AI/ML Product Manager means different things in different organisational contexts. Therefore, it's crucial to grasp the intricacies of the specific role you're interviewing for. This goes beyond a superficial understanding of the job title. It means delving into the job description and deciphering the requirements, expectations, and potential impact of the role within the organisation's broader framework.

The better you understand the role, the better you can align your answers to what the interviewer is looking for.

3. **Research the Company**: Make sure you dive deep into understanding the company's ethos, mission, and products or services. What does the company strive to achieve? What values does it uphold? What is its place in the market? Look for recent news articles or press releases about the company to gather the latest information. It's also beneficial to understand the company's culture to assess your fit. Demonstrating your in-depth knowledge about the company underscores your commitment to the role and the organisation.

4. **Curate Your Questions**: While an interview is a platform for the company to learn about you, it's also an opportunity for you to glean information about the company, role, and team. Prepare thoughtful, insightful questions for your interviewer. Queries could pertain to the work culture, team dynamics, challenges associated with the role, or the company's vision for AI/ML in the coming years. Asking the right questions not only helps you get a clearer picture of whether the role is right for you but it also reinforces your genuine interest in the role and the company.

Mastering the Art of Communication: Essential for the Screening Interview

Embarking on your professional journey into AI/ML product management, the screening interview is your initial gateway to success, your first opportunity to portray your abilities and display your potential. This brief encounter, often limited to 30 minutes or less, can profoundly influence the course of your career trajectory. Here are some critical aspects to focus on:

1. **Adopt a Concise Approach**: Given the time-limited nature of the screening interview, it is crucial to master the art of concise communication. However, being brief doesn't mean compromising on the richness or depth of your responses. Your goal should be to provide comprehensive, well-rounded answers that efficiently capture your skills, experiences, and insights. It's about delivering the maximum impact with the minimum number of words. Keep your answers focused and relevant, avoiding unnecessary digressions. Use this chance to showcase your ability to communicate complex information efficiently – a much sought-after trait in a product manager.

2. **Radiate Genuine Enthusiasm**: Enthusiasm can be a differentiating factor, especially when the technical qualifications among candidates are comparable. Your keen interest in the role, your excitement for the company's mission or product, and your passion

for AI/ML should reverberate in your tone and choice of words. Genuine enthusiasm often signifies commitment, drive, and a positive attitude – traits that are highly valued in dynamic, challenging fields like AI/ML product management.

3. **Prioritise Clarity**: Clarity of speech is paramount, especially for phone or video interviews where visual cues might be absent or limited. This extends beyond merely articulating your words clearly. It also encompasses the coherence of your thoughts, the flow of your narrative, and the way you structure your responses. Ensure your pace is slow enough for your interviewer to follow but not so slow that it hampers the rhythm of the conversation. Strive for a balance between clarity and engagement.

4. **Exemplify Professionalism**: Your communication style should reflect professionalism at all times. Be respectful and attentive, listen actively when your interviewer speaks, and refrain from interrupting. Address your interviewer by their professional title unless they have given you permission to do otherwise. At the end of the interview, express your gratitude for their time and the opportunity. Remember, every interaction, no matter how brief, contributes to the impression you make.

Mastering the art of communication doesn't happen overnight. It's a process that requires practice, self-reflection, and a willingness to adapt and improve. By honing these skills, you'll not only increase your chances of acing the screening interview but also equip yourself for countless professional interactions in your AI/ML product management career.

Anticipating Questions: Key to Excelling in the Screening Interview

Navigating the twists and turns of a screening interview can be an intimidating process. While the precise questions may vary, being prepared for some common inquiries can provide you with the assurance and confidence you need to make a positive impression.

Here are a few questions that frequently arise:

1. **Tell me about yourself**: This open-ended request is often the first one posed, designed to break the ice and set the stage for a more detailed conversation. While it may seem broad, remember to tailor your response to reflect your professional journey. Connect your past experiences, present skills, and future aspirations with a clear focus on your suitability for the role of an AI/ML Product Manager.

2. **Why are you interested in this role/company?**: This question probes your motivation and dedication, enabling the interviewer to gauge whether you're genuinely interested or merely seeking any job. Delve into why you're attracted to the AI/ML field, express your passion for product management, and articulate what aspects of the

company's mission or culture resonate with your professional beliefs and aspirations.

3. **Can you explain your understanding of an AI/ML Product Manager's role?**: This question seeks to verify your comprehension of the role's responsibilities and expectations. It provides an opportunity for you to showcase your industry knowledge and understanding of AI/ML nuances, displaying your preparedness for the role.

4. **Can you talk about your experience with AI/ML projects?**: Your experiences are tangible evidence of your abilities. Use this opportunity to share your most significant achievements, the challenges you faced, and the strategies you used to overcome them. Wherever possible, quantify the impact of your contributions.

5. **Where do you see yourself in five years?**: While this question may seem more personal, it's often asked to assess your ambition, commitment, and long-term planning skills. Be honest but also align your response with the potential growth and opportunities within the role and company.

Each question is a window of opportunity to shine to display your skills, passion, and alignment with the role. Responding confidently and convincingly to these questions requires practice and preparation. Construct potential answers in advance, rehearse them, and try to anticipate the direction the conversation may take based on your responses.

Remember, it's not only about providing the 'correct' answers, but it's also about the assurance and enthusiasm with which you respond. The interviewer is looking to assess not just your technical knowledge and experience but also your communication skills, your commitment to the field, and your cultural fit within the team. Use every question as a platform to portray your well-rounded potential as an AI/ML Product Manager.

The Significance of Post-Interview Etiquette and Reflection

After concluding the interview, your journey towards securing the position as an AI/ML Product Manager continues. While it is tempting to heave a sigh of relief and move on, the period immediately following the interview is crucial to cementing your impression on the interviewer and preparing for subsequent rounds.

Firstly, express gratitude for the opportunity you were given. Sending a thank-you note to the interviewer not only showcases your professional etiquette but also conveys your continued interest in the role. Make this note sincere, personal, and timely—referencing specific aspects of the conversation can help you stand out from the crowd and keep you fresh in the interviewer's mind.

Overcoming the screening interview hurdle is indeed a significant achievement. However, do not let this victory overshadow your sight of the bigger goal. Utilise this period productively to reflect upon the conversation you had.

Record the questions posed to you, the responses you offered, and the instances where you hesitated or felt less confident. Such retrospection provides you with a wealth of insights into your current level of preparedness, helping you identify the areas requiring further work. This process of self-evaluation, though humbling, is key to continual improvement, equipping you for the more complex conversations that lie ahead.

Moreover, if the opportunity arises, seize it to seek feedback from the interviewer. Constructive criticism can serve as an invaluable compass, directing your efforts more effectively towards areas that matter. It offers you an external perspective on your performance, enhancing your understanding of the interviewer's expectations and guiding you towards meeting them.

However, it's essential to approach feedback with the right mindset—see it as a tool for growth rather than a critique of your abilities. The objective is not merely to clear the interview but to evolve through the process, becoming increasingly competent and confident.

The screening interview, while seemingly a small step, is in fact, the first significant milestone in your journey towards the AI/ML Product Manager role. It's akin to the opening act of a concert—setting the tone for the performance to follow. It might appear daunting, especially if you're new to the interview process, but with adequate preparation, reflection, and a positive outlook, it transforms into an enriching experience that draws you closer to your goal.

In summation, the screening interview's success can lay a robust foundation for the subsequent phases of the hiring process. It allows you to present your skills and aspirations, make a personal connection with the interviewer, and express your enthusiasm for the role. Preparing diligently, communicating clearly, and exhibiting a genuine passion for the role are all crucial components of a successful screening interview.

In conclusion, your journey as an aspiring AI/ML Product Manager has truly begun once the screening interview is behind you. The interview's success not only instils confidence but also builds a strong foundation for the subsequent stages of your hiring journey. Thorough preparation, clear communication, and an authentic display of your passion for the role are all integral to making a lasting impression.

Having crossed this initial hurdle, it's time to prepare for the varying interview formats that await you in your pursuit of this dynamic role. The following chapters of this book will introduce these formats and equip you with the necessary strategies to navigate each one effectively. With the screening interview behind you, you have taken a significant leap from 'Zero to Offer'. Remember, 'A good beginning makes a good ending', and having started strong, you are well on your way to achieving your professional goal - landing your dream job as an AI/ML Product Manager.

Let's continue this exciting journey together as we move closer to that coveted offer.

Chapter 11

Acing the Technical Interview

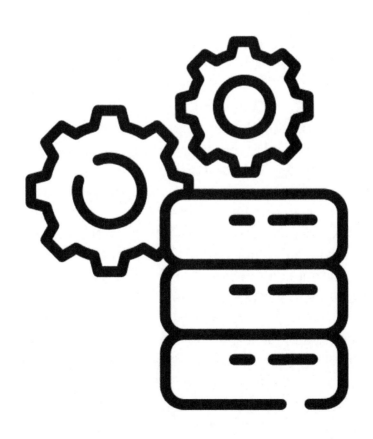

In the realm of AI and Machine Learning, the technical interview is a cornerstone of the recruitment process. This chapter will delve into the intricacies of the technical interview, providing insights into how you can aptly prepare and subsequently excel during this stage of the process.

The AI/ML Product Manager Role: A Unique Intersection

The position of an AI/ML Product Manager is truly distinctive, as it sits squarely at the confluence of several essential disciplines: technology, business, and data science. As a candidate for this role, you are not only expected to have a solid grounding in the fundamentals of Artificial Intelligence (AI) and Machine Learning (ML) but also a deep understanding of business strategy and an ability to leverage data science for strategic decision-making.

When you embark on the journey to becoming an AI/ML Product Manager, you are choosing a path that demands a broad and dynamic skill set. You need to be comfortable working with complex technical concepts and algorithms while also understanding the needs of the business. You are expected to grasp the latest AI and ML trends, translate them into strategic product decisions, and communicate this information effectively to a range of stakeholders, from engineers to senior executives.

During your technical interview, the hiring team will be particularly interested in assessing your technical acumen, your understanding of business strategy in the context of AI/ML, and your grasp of data science principles. But beyond that, they will also be keen to gauge your ability to navigate the dynamic intersection where these disciplines meet. Can you align intricate technical concepts with overarching business objectives? Are you able to leverage your technical knowledge to guide product development while keeping the company's strategic goals in mind? These are the kind of questions they will be looking to answer.

What to Expect in a Technical Interview

To pave the way for your successful AI/ML Product Manager interview journey, it's essential first to demystify what a technical interview usually encompasses. Traditionally, technical interviews serve as an evaluative platform for your understanding of AI and ML algorithms, your proficiency in structuring and solving problems, and your familiarity with software development life cycles, especially within the AI/ML product development landscape.

It's not uncommon for these interviews to delve deep into your knowledge bank of AI and ML. Expect detailed questions around various algorithms and models, their application, strengths, and limitations.

Interviewers will be keen to see whether you can discern which tools and techniques are most appropriate for a given business problem or context.

Problem-solving is another significant aspect of technical interviews. You might be presented with real-world scenarios or hypothetical challenges and be asked to outline your approach to structuring and resolving these problems. The goal here isn't merely to find the 'correct' solution but to assess your thought process, analytical prowess, and resourcefulness.

In addition, a good grasp of the software development life cycle (SDLC) and how it dovetails with AI/ML product development is crucial. You should be comfortable discussing methodologies like Agile or Scrum and understand how AI/ML components fit into different stages of SDLC - from planning and designing to testing and deployment.

Finally, expect to engage in discussions around your experience with current AI/ML product development projects. You may be asked to share examples from your past roles, detailing how you applied your technical skills to contribute to product development.

Preparing for the Interview

As you anticipate the technical interview for an AI/ML Product Manager role, preparation is key. Your preparation should be targeted and robust, focusing on fortifying your technical skills, with a distinct emphasis on AI and ML concepts, proficiency in languages such as Python, R, or Julia, and familiarity with ML libraries like TensorFlow, PyTorch, or sci-kit-learn.

Start by revisiting the core concepts of AI and ML, ensuring your understanding of different machine learning algorithms, deep learning, natural language processing, reinforcement learning, and neural networks is up-to-date and comprehensive. These are not merely academic exercises; the ability to understand and articulate these concepts will be crucial in designing and managing AI/ML-based products.

Next, focus on programming languages common in AI and ML, like Python, R, or Julia. Whether you're coding an ML model from scratch, tweaking an existing model, or simply communicating with your engineering team, your fluency in these languages will prove invaluable. Write code, solve problems, debug errors — the more hands-on you are, the more comfortable you'll become.

Moreover, familiarise yourself with popular ML libraries like TensorFlow, PyTorch, or sci-kit-learn. These tools are widely used in the development and implementation of machine learning models. Understanding how to work with these libraries, the nuances of their syntax, and their strengths and weaknesses can give you a crucial edge.

Don't forget to explore real-world applications and case studies that encapsulate the use of these techniques, languages, and tools. Practical understanding will not only help you relate your learning to the demands of the job but also illustrate your knowledge during the interview.
The more you immerse yourself in this preparation, the better you'll be able to demonstrate your technical proficiency, logical reasoning, and passion for the role during the interview.

Sample AI Product Manager Interview Questions and Answers

1. What is your understanding of an AI/ML Product Manager's role?

Answer: The role of an AI/ML Product Manager is to oversee the development and delivery of AI-powered products. They act as a bridge between the technical (data scientists, ML engineers) and non-technical teams (sales, marketing), translating business needs into technical requirements and vice versa. They have a comprehensive understanding of AI/ML concepts and methodologies, which they use to align product design and development with the company's objectives. They also continuously monitor and evaluate the performance of the product, making adjustments and improvements as needed.

2. Can you describe a project where you used AI/ML to solve a problem?

Answer: Certainly, at my previous job, our team was faced with the challenge of improving the recommendation system for an e-commerce platform. The existing system was relatively basic and didn't account for nuanced customer behaviours. We recognised the potential of ML in this context. As a product manager, I facilitated the collaboration between data scientists, engineers, and business stakeholders to build a new recommendation engine powered by collaborative filtering and matrix factorisation. This model took into account user behaviour and purchase history, vastly improving the relevancy of product recommendations. We saw a significant increase in user engagement and a 20% uplift in sales as a result.

3. How do you manage the trade-off between model performance and complexity in AI/ML products?

Answer: This is a critical aspect of AI/ML product management. While a more complex model might offer marginally better performance, it could be difficult to implement, more prone to errors, and less interpretable. A simpler model might not perform as well, but it could be more reliable, easier to implement, and easier to explain. The right balance depends on the specific context of the product, the technical infrastructure, the skill level of the team, and the needs of the business. It's the Product Manager's job to facilitate discussions around these trade-offs and guide the team towards a decision that aligns with the product goals and business objectives.

4. How do you approach ethical considerations in AI/ML products?

Answer: Ethical considerations should be central to AI/ML product development. As an AI Product Manager, it's essential to consider potential biases in the datasets we use, the fairness and transparency of our algorithms, and the privacy of user data. We need to incorporate ethics checks at every stage of the product life cycle, from the initial concept to ongoing maintenance. For instance, if we find biases in our dataset, we should look for ways to mitigate those biases to ensure fairness. If our model is hard to interpret, we should look for ways to increase transparency, perhaps by incorporating explainability algorithms.

5. What's the biggest challenge you've faced in an AI/ML project, and how did you overcome it?

Answer: The biggest challenge I faced in an AI/ML project was around data quality and availability. We were working on a predictive maintenance model for manufacturing equipment. The challenge was that the data we needed to train the model — failure events — were rare, and the existing data was inconsistent.

To overcome this, I coordinated with our data engineers to implement better data collection and processing protocols. We also used synthetic data generation techniques to balance our dataset. We combined these methods with an anomaly detection approach to the model, which better suited the available data. In the end, we were able to develop a predictive maintenance model that significantly reduced unexpected equipment downtime.

6. How would you explain a complex AI/ML concept, like overfitting, to a non-technical stakeholder?

Answer: Overfitting is like studying for an exam by memorising the answers to past papers. You might do well if the questions in the real exam happen to be the same as the ones you've memorised. But if the questions are even slightly different, you won't perform well because you've not really understood the subject — you've just memorised specific answers. Similarly, an overfitted model has 'memorised' the training data. It performs well on that data but not on new, unseen data because it hasn't truly 'understood' the underlying patterns.

7. How would you prioritise features in an AI/ML product?

Answer: Prioritising features in an AI/ML product should be a strategic decision based on several factors. These include the impact on the product goals, the complexity of implementation, the resource availability, and the urgency from stakeholders. I usually start by defining the impact and effort of each feature, often using a framework like RICE (Reach, Impact, Confidence, Effort). Then, I align these findings with the product's goals and the company's strategy. This process should also include consultations with the different stakeholders, including the technical team (who will build the feature), the business team (who might use or sell the product), and of course, the users (who will ultimately use the feature).

8. Can you describe a time when you had to make a difficult decision about an AI/ML product?

Answer: In a previous role, we were developing a personalised marketing product using natural language processing. However, during the development process, the data scientists found that the model was potentially infringing on user privacy because of the type of data it was processing. Despite the promising results from the initial tests, I made the decision to halt the project temporarily. We then worked with our legal and compliance teams to perform a thorough review of the data usage and the potential privacy implications. It was a challenging decision, as it delayed our project timeline, but it was essential to ensure we respected our users' privacy and complied with all regulations.

9. How do you measure success in AI/ML products?

Answer: The success of an AI/ML product should be measured by how well it achieves its intended goal. For a recommendation engine, this might be an increase in click-through rate or a higher average order value. For a predictive maintenance model, this might be a decrease in machine downtime. The key is to identify the right metrics that align with the product's objective and the business's goals. However, we should also monitor the AI/ML model's performance metrics, like accuracy, precision, recall, and F1 score, to ensure the model is performing as expected.

10. What is your approach to working with a diverse team that includes data scientists, engineers, and business professionals?

Answer: Working with a diverse team requires excellent communication and collaboration skills. Each team member brings a unique perspective, and as a Product Manager, my role is to facilitate the collaboration of these perspectives towards a shared goal. This requires understanding each team's language — the technical language of data scientists and engineers and the business language of the professionals. I continuously strive to keep the lines of communication open, making sure each team understands the product goals and their role in achieving them. By fostering a collaborative environment, we can ensure that everyone's expertise is utilised, leading to a successful product.

By having well-prepared answers to these questions, you can show your technical understanding, your problem-solving abilities, and your team management skills — all essential for a successful AI/ML Product Manager.

Translating Technical Knowledge

The essentiality of technical knowledge within the AI/ML domain is unquestionable, forming a pivotal part of your toolset as a Product Manager. However, it is equally important to remember that the position you're interviewing for is not that of a data scientist or a machine learning engineer but a Product Manager. Hence, this role's crux demands a unique ability to meld technical and business worlds coherently.

As an AI/ML Product Manager, your primary responsibility extends beyond the realm of the algorithmic labyrinth. You're positioned at the unique intersection where business goals intertwine with technical feasibility, and it's your responsibility to communicate and translate complex, often abstract, technical concepts into language digestible by various stakeholders.

These stakeholders, including senior management, marketing teams, sales personnel, or even customers, may lack the in-depth technical understanding that you possess. This lack, however, does not diminish their interest or stake in the project's outcome. Your ability to effectively interpret and communicate the implications of a particular algorithm, the choice between different ML models, or the trade-offs of adopting one technical approach over another in a clear, concise, and impactful manner forms an essential part of your role.

Striking this balance between deep technical comprehension and articulate business communication is what makes an AI/ML Product Manager a successful conduit between the technical team and the rest of the company, ensuring that the technical developments contribute directly to achieving business objectives.

Mock Interviews and Communication Practice

Mock interviews hold a powerful role in the interview preparation process. They serve as a practical training ground where you can fine-tune your responses, gauge your performance, and, most importantly, gain valuable insights into the areas requiring further improvement. Regularly engaging in mock interviews with peers or utilising online platforms that offer such facilities can familiarise you with the potential questions that interviewers might pose.

The practice of mock interviews is not just about answering the questions correctly but also about how you convey those answers. Succinct, clear, and confident communication is pivotal. It can differentiate you from other candidates possessing similar technical know-how. These simulated interview scenarios offer you the space to master the skill of being concise yet comprehensive, a valued trait in the fast-paced corporate world.

Another invaluable skill that can be honed through mock interviews is the ability to articulate complex technical concepts in a simple, digestible manner. You could extend your practice by explaining AI/ML concepts to friends or family members who don't possess technical expertise. This exercise will challenge you to break down complex ideas into understandable chunks, a skill that will certainly give you an edge in the actual interview.

In essence, mock interviews are a safe space for trial and error, for refining your approach, and for receiving constructive feedback. The goal is not just about rehearsing but gaining confidence, improving articulation, and, above all, learning how to manage nerves under simulated pressure. These mock trials, though not a guarantee of success, significantly improve your chances of delivering a memorable performance when it truly counts.

Showcasing Your Problem-Solving Skills

At the heart of a technical interview, especially for a position such as an AI/ML Product Manager, lies the evaluation of problem-solving skills. Whilst knowledge and proficiency in specific areas are undoubtedly important, the ability to apply that knowledge in tackling real-world problems is of paramount importance.

In a dynamic field like AI and ML, challenges are abundant and often multifaceted. The interviewer's aim is to assess the breadth of your knowledge and your capability to logically dissect a problem, hypothesise potential solutions, and methodically chart a path towards resolution.

How you approach a problem, your thought process, and the strategies you deploy to break down complex issues into manageable parts form the crux of what the hiring team is keen to observe. They are interested in seeing your analytical thinking in action - how you scrutinise the problem from various angles, discern the core issues, and generate effective, innovative solutions.

Moreover, your ability to adapt when a chosen solution doesn't work as anticipated is another critical aspect that interviewers look for. It reveals resilience, flexibility and tenacity - all highly desirable traits in an AI/ML Product Manager. The interview, therefore, becomes a platform to not only showcase your technical prowess but also to demonstrate how you can employ these skills to navigate complex, problem-solving scenarios.

Understanding the Ethical Implications

In the exciting and fast-paced domain of Artificial Intelligence and Machine Learning, one aspect that stands to be equally vital as the technological facets understand the ethical implications of AI and ML products. This holds especially true for an AI/ML Product Manager role, which requires a holistic approach to product development and management.

The advancement of AI and ML technologies has brought forth a myriad of ethical questions revolving around fairness, accountability, transparency, and privacy. These questions emerge because AI/ML systems, despite being highly efficient, can inadvertently perpetuate biases, infringe privacy, or make decisions that lack transparency.

As an AI/ML Product Manager, you will find yourself in a unique position to shape the development and deployment of these technologies. It is crucial that you possess a firm understanding of these potential ethical pitfalls. You should be aware of how biased data can lead to skewed algorithms, how this can further amplify existing societal inequalities, and how you can employ measures to mitigate such biases.

Additionally, you will need to be cognizant of privacy issues that can arise with the use of sensitive data. You should know how to balance the benefits of personalised user experience, which requires data, against the potential privacy risks. Transparency is another ethical dimension that you should be well-versed in - the ability to explain AI/ML models' decisions is critical for fostering trust and ensuring fairness.

In essence, your role as an AI/ML Product Manager demands that you not only have a robust understanding of AI/ML technologies, but also the ethical implications that come with their deployment. This dual understanding will enable you to guide product development in a way that maximises the benefits of AI/ML while also adhering to the highest ethical standards.

The Importance of 'How' Over 'What'

In the context of technical interviews, particularly for AI/ML Product Manager roles, it's crucial to understand that the process is as much about the 'how' as it is about the 'what'. While interviewers indeed pay attention to your answers, they're equally—if not more—interested in observing how you arrive at them.

The journey you take to reach a solution often provides valuable insights into your thought process, analytical skills, and problem-solving approach, which are all indispensable qualities for a Product Manager. It's through the 'how' that interviewers can gauge your ability to dissect complex issues, apply logical reasoning, and devise effective solutions.

For instance, if you're presented with a challenging problem, do you dive straight into solutions, or do you take a moment to understand its nuances? Do you ask clarifying questions to ensure you've grasped the problem fully? Are you methodical in your approach, breaking the problem into smaller, manageable parts? Can you think critically, evaluate multiple perspectives, and weigh the pros and cons of potential solutions?
Moreover, the 'how' can also demonstrate your communication skills.

Being able to walk the interviewer through your thought process in a clear and coherent manner is vital. It not only evidences your technical understanding, but it also showcases your ability to communicate complex ideas effectively—a must-have skill in the realm of product management.

Cultural Fit: An Essential Factor

In the recruitment process, especially for product manager roles within AI/ML domains, 'fit' with the company culture is often as critical as technical expertise. This aspect of the selection process goes beyond your credentials and experience, reaching into the essence of who you are as a professional and how well you'll blend with the existing team dynamics and company ethos.

Interviewers aren't merely looking for technically proficient candidates; they're also seeking individuals who share the company's values, align with its mission, and can contribute positively to its unique workplace culture. Whether it's a startup fostering an environment of innovation and risk-taking or a corporate entity that prioritises structure and established procedures, each organisation has its distinctive culture. As such, your ability to integrate and thrive in this environment is paramount.

Moreover, interviewers are keen to discern if you're someone they, and the broader team, would enjoy working with on a day-to-day basis. As a product manager, your role will involve interacting with many individuals from various departments, necessitating effective communication and teamwork skills and a positive and collaborative attitude.

Therefore, it's important during the interview process to convey not only your capabilities as a professional but also your personality, values, and working style. Remember to be yourself, and let your interpersonal skills shine through. After all, it's your unique blend of skills, experiences, and attributes that can make you the perfect cultural fit for the company.

Conclusion
In conclusion, the technical interview is critical to the AI/ML PM interview process. By effectively preparing, honing your technical and communication skills, and demonstrating a structured approach to problem-solving, you can succeed

in this stage and be one step closer to landing your dream role as an AI/ML Product Manager.

In the next chapters of this book, we will walk through further stages of the AI/ML PM interview process, providing tips and strategies to help you succeed. By preparing adequately for each stage of the process, you can turn every interview into an opportunity, getting closer and closer to receiving your coveted job offer. Good luck, and remember: the journey from zero to offer is a learning experience in itself, one that will help you grow as a professional and as an individual.

Chapter 12

The Behavioural Interview

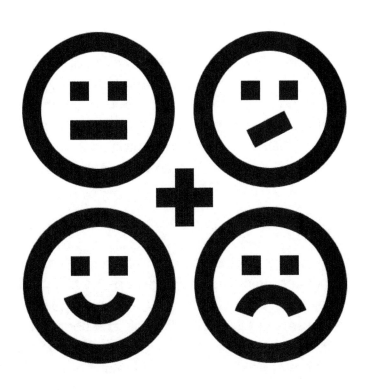

In the dynamic, high-stakes world of Artificial Intelligence (AI) and Machine Learning (ML), your technical prowess may lay the foundation, but it is your interpersonal competencies that truly define your success.

As a professional in this field, you aren't merely dealing with abstract algorithms and vast datasets; you are, in fact, managing intricate products, coordinating multifaceted teams, and influencing organisational direction. Your every decision could potentially instigate a seismic shift in the technological landscape. This underlines the vital importance of possessing robust people skills in such a role.

As we delve into this chapter, we shall venture beyond the complexities of code and computations and into the realm of Behavioural Interviews. These aren't casual conversations about your past experiences and work preferences. Rather, they are methodical and focused examinations of your past behaviour to indicate your future actions.

Our journey through this chapter will equip you with an understanding of this nuanced aspect of the hiring process, arming you with the insights and strategies necessary to navigate these interviews with finesse and confidence. The focus will be on transforming this potentially daunting exercise into a rewarding opportunity to shine a spotlight on your unique blend of skills and attributes, thereby maximising your chances of securing your desired AI/ML Product Manager role.

The Nature of Behavioural Interviews:

Shedding the casualness often associated with discussions about one's experiences and work style, Behavioural Interviews introduce a systematic, focused methodology to the conversation. They are a structured process designed not merely to delve into the past but to extrapolate from it, gleaning insights about how you might manoeuvre future scenarios.

Though it may seem paradoxical, given the context of AI and ML, the emphasis in Behavioural Interviews is decidedly human-centric. Here, your technical knowledge of AI and ML, while important, takes a backseat. Instead, the spotlight shines brightly on your problem-solving acumen, your ability to articulate and communicate, your leadership style, and how well you fit into the company's culture.

The essence of Behavioural Interviews lies in their inherent philosophy: the notion that past behaviours are often reliable predictors of future performance. As a candidate, you are expected to demonstrate not what you know but how you apply your knowledge and skills in real-world contexts. It is about dissecting past situations to understand your thinking patterns, decision-making processes, and behavioural responses, all of which are considered indicative of how you would tackle similar challenges in the future.

In short, Behavioural Interviews go beyond the superficial layer of skills and experiences, aiming to unravel the complex tapestry of traits, attitudes, and behaviours that define you as a professional. They offer a unique lens through which potential employers can get a glimpse of the 'real you', ultimately aiding them in making informed decisions about your suitability for the organisation and the role at hand.

Preparation:

As with any significant endeavour, acing a behavioural interview necessitates thorough preparation. Unlike technical interviews, where you might focus on honing specific technical skills, preparation for behavioural interviews is akin to refining an art – the art of storytelling.

In a behavioural interview, you're the protagonist of your narrative, and your experiences are the intricate plot elements that help weave a compelling tale. This narrative serves to highlight your professional journey, underscoring the skills you've acquired, the challenges you've overcome, and the accomplishments you've achieved.

But weaving an engaging tale requires skill and practice. The ability to distil your experiences into clear, concise, and captivating narratives is paramount. This involves filtering the most relevant incidents from your past, recollecting the critical details, and presenting them in an organised and coherent manner. Your stories should effortlessly thread together the situation, the challenges, your actions, and the subsequent results.

Moreover, it's crucial to remember that your narrative needs to resonate with your interviewers. Understanding the job description, the role requirements and the company's culture can help you tailor your stories accordingly, thereby enhancing their relevance and impact.

But preparation for a behavioural interview doesn't stop at just crafting compelling narratives. It also involves anticipating potential questions, reflecting on your career highs and lows, and being prepared to discuss them with honesty and introspection.

Additionally, it's essential to strike a balance between being detailed in your responses and being succinct. Going too deep into the minutiae might risk losing the interviewer's attention, while being overly brief may not fully showcase your skills and experiences.

Lastly, remember that successful preparation also includes being mentally ready for the interview. Approach it with confidence, maintain a positive attitude, and keep in mind that it's an opportunity to share your professional journey, the lessons you've learned, and how these have shaped you into the professional you are today.

The STAR Method:

The STAR method, standing for Situation, Task, Action, and Result, is an instrumental storytelling tool that can assist you in structuring your responses during a behavioural interview.

Serving as a guide, the STAR method takes the interviewer on a journey that starts with a specific 'Situation' you have faced. This forms the backdrop of your story, and it is in your interest to choose a scenario that is pertinent to the role for which you're being interviewed. The situation might stem from a past professional role, academic project, or even a personal incident that illuminates your problem-solving prowess.

Next, you delineate the 'Task' at hand. In essence, this section should shed light on the responsibilities you held in the given situation, the objectives that were set, and the challenges you anticipated. It is essential to articulate these tasks clearly, highlighting the complexities without delving into unnecessary technical jargon.

Following the exposition of the task, you describe the 'Action' that you took to overcome the situation. This portion provides you with the opportunity to spotlight your problem-solving skills, strategic thinking, and adaptability. You ought to focus on your personal contributions and decisions and detail how you navigated the challenges encountered.

Lastly, you share the 'Result' - the outcome of your actions. This is where you can showcase the impact of your actions. Quantify your achievements where possible, be it in terms of efficiency gains, cost savings, or team milestones reached. Equally, don't shy away from sharing the lessons learned and how the experience contributed to your professional growth.

By applying the STAR method, you ensure that your narrative is structured, comprehensive, and compelling. It assists you in articulating your past experiences and achievements, leaving a lasting impression on your interviewer. This technique can be a powerful tool, turning a potentially abstract conversation into a sequence of meaningful and measurable events that effectively demonstrate your capabilities.

Tailoring Your Stories:

While the STAR method provides a structure for your responses, the substance of your narratives is equally critical. Tailoring your stories to the specific role you're applying for can make a world of difference to your behavioural interview performance.

To begin with, analyse the job description in detail. Understand the responsibilities, skills, qualifications, and experiences that the employer values. Make a note of key attributes, such as leadership, problem-solving, adaptability, or communication skills, and carefully select experiences that display these competencies.

Next, consider the context of the organisation. Do they prize innovation or respect tradition? Are they risk-takers or more risk-averse? These cultural aspects can inform the type of narratives you select. For instance, a story about implementing a disruptive technology might resonate more with a startup, while a tale about steering a project through rigorous compliance standards might strike a chord with a larger, more traditional firm.

Furthermore, consider the specific challenges of the industry and role. If you're interviewing for a position in AI and ML, you might tell stories that highlight your ability to navigate ethical complexities, manage large data sets, or liaise between technical and non-technical teams.

The stories you tell in a behavioural interview should not merely be a chronicle of your past experiences. They should be carefully selected, adapted, and presented in a way that convinces the interviewer that you possess the skills, mindset, and cultural alignment that make you the right fit for the role. Tailoring your narratives in this way not only reveals your understanding of the role and the company but also helps you make a memorable, meaningful connection with your interviewer.

Types of Questions:

While every behavioural interview may vary slightly in its specifics, there are certain patterns and categories that questions often fall into, and understanding these can greatly enhance your preparation. These questions are designed to probe into various aspects of your thinking, decision-making processes, and overall ability to handle situations.

A significant category of questions focuses on your problem-solving abilities. You might be asked to describe a time when you overcame a major hurdle at work, came up with an innovative solution to a problem, or turned a failing project around. These questions are designed to uncover your ability to identify issues, think critically, and apply effective strategies to reach a resolution.

Another category of questions is centred around teamwork and interpersonal skills. Interviewers often ask about your experiences in a team setting, dealing with a difficult team member, or leading a group towards a shared goal. These questions aim to gauge your ability to work with others, your leadership style, and your negotiation skills.

In addition, you may also face questions about how you handle pressure and adapt to change. Interviewers may ask about times when you had to manage stress, adapt to an unexpected change, or balance multiple high-priority tasks. These queries are meant to assess your resilience, adaptability, and time management skills.

Lastly, questions about your motivation and values are also common in behavioural interviews. These could be questions about what motivates you, how you align your work with your values, or instances where you had to make a difficult ethical decision. These questions offer insights into your intrinsic motivation, ethical grounding, and cultural fit with the company.

Understanding these types of questions and having thought-out, tailored responses ready can go a long way in elevating your performance in a behavioural interview. Remember, the goal is to illustrate how your experiences, skills, and mindset align with the role you're applying for.

10 Behavioural Questions and Example Answers

Behavioural interview questions offer an opportunity to provide a window into your personality, capabilities, and experiences. As an AI Product Manager, being able to answer these questions effectively will showcase your ability to lead teams, drive product vision, handle challenging situations, and embody the cultural ethos of the organisation. This chapter presents ten potential behavioural questions you may encounter in an interview and provides example answers to help guide your responses.

- **Can you tell us about a time when you faced a significant challenge on a product and how did you overcome it?**

Example answer: During my previous role, we faced significant delays due to unforeseen technical challenges in integrating AI capabilities into our product. Recognising the potential impact on the product launch timeline, I organised a brainstorming session with the technical team. Together, we identified the core problem and developed a revised plan to ensure the integration happened smoothly without compromising the product's functionality. This experience taught me the value of cross-functional collaboration and the importance of problem-solving in a time-sensitive environment.

- **How do you prioritise features for a product?**

Example answer: Prioritising features involves a delicate balance between customer needs, business objectives, and technical feasibility. I use a scoring system based on these factors to rank potential features. This allows me to create a prioritised roadmap that aligns with our strategic goals. I also maintain open lines of communication with all stakeholders to ensure the roadmap reflects evolving needs and expectations.

- **Describe a time you had to manage a conflict within your team.**

Example answer: In one project, two of my team members had conflicting views on the technical approach to an ML model. Both perspectives were valuable, but the disagreement was causing delays. I organised a meeting where each member could present their viewpoint, focusing on the benefits and potential drawbacks of each approach. Following the discussion, the team agreed to experiment with both methods on smaller scales to gather data and make an informed decision. This experience highlighted the importance of communication and data-driven decision-making in resolving conflicts.

- **Can you share an instance where you had to make a tough decision that didn't please everyone?**

Example answer: In one project, due to a sudden change in market trends, it was clear that our initial product direction would not meet the customers' needs. Despite resistance from some team members, I decided to pivot our product direction based on the new market data. While it was a challenging decision, it ultimately led to a more relevant and successful product. This taught me that making the right decision requires courage and conviction, even in the face of opposition.

- **How do you handle feedback, and can you share an example of when you acted on feedback?**

Example answer: I believe feedback is crucial for personal and professional growth. In my last role, my manager suggested that I could improve my presentation skills to better convey our product's value to non-technical stakeholders. I took this on board and enrolled in a professional communication course. The improvement in my ability to explain complex AI concepts in simple terms increased stakeholder engagement significantly, leading to more informed decision-making across the board.

- **Tell us about a time you had to adapt quickly to a new situation.**

Example answer: In my previous role, our company was acquired by a larger organisation. This brought many changes in processes, tools, and team structure. I took it upon myself to quickly learn the new systems, adapt to the modified reporting structures, and help my team navigate through this transition. This experience helped me develop resilience and reinforced the importance of adaptability in the face of change.

- **How have you ensured ethical considerations in your AI/ML product development?**

Example answer: In one project, we were developing a facial recognition system. I pushed for a thorough review of the ethical implications, given the potential privacy concerns. I insisted on incorporating an 'opt-out' feature for users who didn't want to participate and made sure our data collection and usage were transparent. I believe ethical considerations should be integral to AI/ML products to ensure trust and respect for user privacy.

- **Can you describe a time when you influenced others to support your product vision?**

Example answer: I once had a product vision that involved leveraging a new but relatively unproven AI technology. There was initial resistance due to perceived risks. I held workshops to educate the team on the technology, highlighting its potential impact and the ways we could mitigate risks. Over time, I was able to build consensus and steer the team towards my vision, resulting in a cutting-edge product that gave us a significant market advantage.

- **Tell us about a time when you used data to make a decision.**

Example answer: During the development of an AI tool, we had different opinions about the direction of the user interface design. To resolve the conflict, I proposed conducting A/B testing to gather user feedback on the design options. The data collected made it clear which design was more user-friendly and helped us make an informed decision that everyone could get behind.

- **How do you handle setbacks?**

Example answer: Setbacks are part of the product development journey, especially in the AI/ML space. When a setback occurs, I first focus on understanding the cause. I then rally the team to find potential solutions, ensuring that every setback is viewed as a learning opportunity. For instance, when an AI product failed during beta testing, I led the team in identifying the issue, reworking the model, and successfully delivering a more robust product.

Common Pitfalls:

A common pitfall in behavioural interviews is being too vague or generic in your responses. Be specific and use tangible outcomes to demonstrate your skills and accomplishments.

Reflection and Practice:

Contemplation and practice are integral aspects of preparing for a behavioural interview. As an AI product manager, your experiences, work style, values, and career goals form the very fabric of your professional persona. Taking the time to reflect on these can not only provide you with a stockpile of compelling stories to share but also offer a deeper understanding of who you are as a professional.

Reflection begins with a thorough introspection into your past experiences. Revisit the projects you've worked on, the teams you've been a part of, the challenges you've overcome, and the successes you've enjoyed. Each of these instances could contain powerful narratives that can underscore your skills and highlight your competencies.

Remember, it's not always about the big wins; sometimes, stories about overcoming minor glitches, handling a difficult team member, or demonstrating perseverance can also effectively exhibit your problem-solving abilities, leadership skills, and resilience.

Understanding your work style, on the other hand, is about identifying how you operate best. Are you a lone wolf who thrives on autonomy, or do you find synergy in a team? Are you a visionary with an eye on the big picture, or do you excel in executing details? Such insights not only help you articulate your strengths in an interview but also allow you to assess if the role aligns with your work style.

Furthermore, identifying your values and career goals is crucial. Your values act as your compass, guiding your decisions and actions, while your career goals provide a roadmap for your professional journey.

Knowing these allows you to align your stories with the company's ethos and communicate your long-term commitment to the role and the industry.

Practice, the other side of this coin, is about rehearsing your responses. It involves tailoring your narratives to match the job requirements, refining your storytelling to ensure clarity and engagement, and getting comfortable with voicing your thoughts. The more you practice, the more confident you'll become, turning your interview into a platform to showcase your uniqueness as an AI product manager.

The Two-Way Street:

It's crucial to remember that a behavioural interview isn't a one-sided evaluation. Yes, you're under the microscope, but this is also your chance to ascertain if the company is a good fit for you. In essence, a behavioural interview is a two-way street, a dialogue where you also have the freedom to ask questions and gain insight into the organisation's culture, values, and modus operandi.

This exercise is particularly important for the role of an AI product manager, a position steeped in collaboration, strategy, and vision. You must determine whether the organisation's culture supports your working style and nurtures innovation. Is it a flat structure promoting open communication and cross-departmental cooperation, or does it adhere to traditional hierarchies? Understanding the cultural fabric of the organisation can provide vital clues about your potential success and satisfaction in the role.

Additionally, the company's values should align with your personal ethos. If you're passionate about responsible AI, for instance, you'd want to ensure that the organisation also emphasises ethical AI development.

Finally, the way of working is another aspect to consider. Is the company agile, with a fast-paced environment that values quick decision-making? Or does it prefer a more methodical, measured approach?

Don't hesitate to ask questions about these elements. You might query about the company's approach to AI ethics or the working dynamic between product managers and other teams. A robust understanding of these facets can help you make an informed decision about the company, ensuring a productive and fulfilling tenure as an AI product manager.

Remember, a job interview isn't just about them choosing you; it's also about you choosing them.

Being Likeable:

An element often glossed over in the rigour of behavioural interviews is the necessity of being likeable. Although the interview room might feel like a stage for your professional prowess, it's equally an arena to showcase your personality to display that you're not just a cog in the machine but a vibrant individual capable of establishing warm, collaborative relationships.

In a field as interactive and dynamic as AI product management, your technical aptitude may get you through the door, but it's your ability to forge meaningful relationships, to connect on a personal level that truly makes a difference. After all, as a product manager, you'll work closely with many stakeholders - from engineers and designers to marketing professionals and customers. Being personable, likeable, and approachable is crucial.

So, when faced with behavioural interview questions, remember to project warmth, authenticity, and genuine interest besides demonstrating your problem-solving abilities or leadership skills. Pay attention to the interviewer, actively listen, and respond with consideration. Show enthusiasm for the role and the company.

- 1. Consider adding more specific examples to illustrate the points being made in the text. This would make the information more relatable and easier to understand for the reader.

- Include more practical tips on how to prepare for a behavioural interview, such as specific techniques for crafting compelling narratives and anticipating potential questions. This would make the text more actionable and useful for the reader.

Maintain eye contact, smile where appropriate, and express your thoughts clearly. Establishing this personal connection can differentiate you from equally qualified candidates. It could well be the difference between 'almost there' and 'welcome aboard'. Remember, people often forget what you said or did, but they never forget how you made them feel. So, let your innate charisma shine through and make your behavioural interview a memorable one.

Conclusion:

Behavioural interviews seem daunting because they delve into the realms of your experiences and personality. However, they present a unique opportunity to demonstrate your unique blend of skills, experiences, and attributes. Use the advice in this chapter to turn your behavioural interview into a persuasive performance that paints a vivid picture of you as an exceptional AI/ML Product Manager.

Relevance Across Roles and Industries:

Bear in mind that while this chapter has focused on interviews for AI/ML Product Management roles, the principles are broadly applicable across roles and industries. As more organisations embrace behavioural interviews as part of their hiring process, mastering this form of the interview will serve you well throughout your career.

Part IV

Interviewing Mastery

Mastering the interviewing process is a crucial factor in progressing your career within the AI & ML industry. It is not simply about responding to questions adequately but about showcasing your skills, knowledge, and aptitude for the product manager role in a way that sets you apart from other candidates.

1. Understanding the Interviewer's Perspective

Remember, the person interviewing you is not just checking off a list of qualifications and skills. They are looking for the best fit for their team and organisation, and their assessment will be subjective and nuanced. They will consider aspects such as your communication skills, how you deal with pressure, and whether you exhibit the problem-solving capabilities critical for a PM role in AI/ML.

2. Developing a Strong Narrative

Every question is an opportunity to tell a story about your experiences and skills. Develop a compelling narrative that illustrates your unique career journey, detailing how it has led you to this point and why you are a strong candidate for the role.

3. Technical Proficiency

Technical expertise is a cornerstone for any product manager in AI/ML. Be ready to showcase your understanding of key AI/ML concepts and tools. Explain how you have used these tools to drive project success, address challenges, and generate results.

4. Demonstrating Business Acumen

Having an understanding of the wider business environment is critical. You must show that you can apply your AI/ML knowledge in a way that aligns with the company's strategy and contributes to its bottom line.

5. Showcasing Leadership and Teamwork

Product management is a role that straddles multiple teams and disciplines. Being able to work with diverse teams, lead initiatives, and manage conflicts is a necessity. Provide examples of your ability to lead and collaborate.

6. Exhibit Curiosity and Learning

The field of AI and ML is rapidly evolving. Demonstrate your ability to learn, adapt, and stay abreast of industry developments. Show your commitment to self-improvement and lifelong learning.

7. Preparing for Different Interview Formats

Be prepared for different types of interviews, such as behavioural, case study, and technical interviews. Each has its format and requires a different approach and preparation.

8. Mastering the Art of Follow-up

The process doesn't end with the interview. Follow up professionally, expressing your appreciation for the opportunity to interview and reaffirming your interest in the role.

9. Handling Rejections

Not every interview will result in a job offer. Learn to handle rejections gracefully. Seek feedback, learn from it, and use it to improve your future performance.

10. Continuous Improvement

Interviewing is a skill, and like any skill, it can be improved with practice. Always look for opportunities to hone your interviewing skills. Take every interview as a learning experience.

Remember, mastering interviews is a journey. Take it one step at a time, and don't be disheartened by the obstacles along the way. With persistence and practice, you will see progress and eventually land your desired AI/ML PM role.

Chapter 13

The Case Study Interview

Case study interviews maintain a substantial role in the selection process for AI/ML Product Manager positions. Far from being rudimentary exercises designed to gauge your capability to grapple with complex issues, these interviews actually serve as microcosms of real-world scenarios that you are likely to face in your professional environment. As such, these interviews become an effective platform to demonstrate your skills and potential. The unique blend of business conundrums, technical facets, and data-driven decision-making instances encountered in these case study interviews mimic the multifaceted challenges of the AI/ML industry.

The beauty of these interviews lies in their authenticity and relevance to the job role. As candidates, you aren't just walking through a series of hypothetical problems but rather engaging with instances that resemble the kind of issues you'll be tackling once you're part of the organisation. This realistic approach grants a dual advantage - it offers the interviewer an accurate gauge of your problem-solving abilities, and simultaneously, it provides you, as a prospective AI/ML product manager, with a sneak peek into the dynamics of the role. The crux of these interviews lies in their ability to portray a realistic picture of the intricate amalgam of business, technical, and data-oriented decision-making challenges that define the AI/ML landscape.

Understanding the Role:

Sometimes, candidates can feel daunted by the breadth and depth of knowledge seemingly necessary to navigate these case study interviews effectively. It may seem like an insurmountable task to be an expert in every facet of AI and ML technologies. However, one must remember that the role of a product manager isn't about achieving mastery in AI/ML. Rather, it focuses on understanding the nuanced implications of these technologies, identifying appropriate use cases, and working seamlessly with other teams to ensure successful product development and management.

The role requires a degree of technical understanding, but more significantly, it necessitates an ability to translate that technical understanding into viable product strategies. The product manager operates at the intersection of technology and business strategy, which means the ability to see the bigger picture, identify opportunities and challenges, and steer the product development process towards success.

This means that you need not be the person designing the algorithms but the one who comprehends their impacts, sees where they fit within the product roadmap, and collaborates efficiently across departments, tying together the various strands that weave the fabric of an effective AI/ML product.

In essence, the product manager's role is about synergy - bringing together technical comprehension and business acumen, connecting people and processes, and marrying innovation with practicality to drive product success. Understanding this can ease the pressure of feeling the need to know everything about AI/ML and instead help you focus on the bigger picture - delivering value through effective product management.

A Structured Approach:

Excelling in case study interviews necessitates adopting a structured and systematic approach. Your journey towards crafting a solution commences with a clear and thorough comprehension of the problem statement. It's important not to rush this step; take your time to truly understand the crux of the problem. If anything is ambiguous or unclear, don't hesitate to ask clarifying questions. Remember, the interviewer will be observing your ability to ask insightful questions as much as they will be assessing your problem-solving skills.

Once you've acquired a clear understanding of the problem, proceed to break it down into manageable, digestible parts. This dissection not only aids in promoting clear and organised thinking but it also makes the overall task seem less intimidating. It's akin to solving a complex puzzle, where addressing each piece individually eventually leads to the completion of the whole picture.

Having broken down the problem, move on to brainstorming potential solutions for each individual part. This is where your understanding of AI/ML, your knowledge of the current market trends, your insights into customer behaviour, and your awareness of the company's context come into play. Remember, it's not about finding the perfect solution right away but exploring different paths and strategies. This approach allows you to examine the problem from various angles and helps in generating creative, practical, and effective solutions.

In essence, adopting a structured approach to solving case study problems ensures you remain focused and organised. It gives you the room to think deeply and critically about the problem at hand while also facilitating the effective communication of your thought process and final solution.

Clear Articulation:

Your clarity of expression throughout the process carries weight. This reflects your ability to effectively communicate complex information, an essential skill for a product manager. Resist the urge to leap to solutions hastily; the journey to the solution is as critical as the solution itself. Ethical Considerations:

The AI/ML landscape also necessitates a keen awareness of ethical considerations. Issues surrounding data privacy, fairness, and transparency should be integral to your discussion, exhibiting your understanding of AI/ML and its societal implications.

Practice:

Practice forms the bedrock of excellence in case study interviews. Immersing oneself in a wide spectrum of case studies can help develop a familiarity with the format, a refinement of problem-solving skills, and a growth in self-confidence. The more one is exposed to varied scenarios, the better equipped one becomes to tackle the unexpected and think on their feet. This practice aids in developing agility and flexibility in thought, which is paramount in navigating the often unpredictable landscape of AI/ML problems.

Case study interviews are unique in that they put your theoretical knowledge to the test in practical scenarios. They provide a simulated environment where you can demonstrate how your understanding of AI/ML can be leveraged to solve real-world problems. The more you practice, the more proficient you become in applying your knowledge, making connections, and deriving solutions.

Understanding Case Presentation Formats:

In the realm of case study interviews, the problem can be presented to the interviewee in a multitude of formats. It could be a verbal case where the interviewer describes a situation, and you are expected to ask probing questions and propose solutions. It might also be a written case study, where you are given some time to review a document detailing the problem, and the discussion commences post-review.

In some cases, companies have been known to send the case study a few days before the interview, providing you ample time to prepare a presentation for the discussion. Regardless of the format, the underlying principle remains consistent; your aptitude to dissect complex problems and devise solutions within an AI/ML context is what's being put to the test.

Examining from User, Business, and Technical Perspectives:

When dissecting the problem, a holistic view is crucial. The user should be at the heart of your analysis. Understanding the user's perspective, their challenges, and their needs can inform your problem analysis. A product's purpose is, ultimately, to cater to a user's needs or solve their problems, making a user-centric approach essential to successful problem-solving.

Following this, the business perspective should come into focus. It's imperative to consider the sustainability of the product within the company's business goals. This involves understanding the market landscape, the competition, and the unique selling propositions of the company.

Finally, but importantly, the technical perspective mustn't be overlooked. Given that you are bridging the gap between the technical and non-technical teams, your understanding of AI/ML's capabilities and limitations is crucial. However, you are not expected to propose specific algorithms or technical solutions. Rather, your role would be to identify potential areas where AI/ML could add value and suggest how it could be integrated into the product.

Maintaining a Logical Flow and Coherent Structure:

Throughout your response, maintaining a logical flow and coherent structure is important. This aids not only your thought process but also makes it easier for the interviewer to follow your line of thinking. Using established frameworks such as SWOT analysis, Porter's Five Forces, or even a simple pro and con list can help maintain a structured response.

Moreover, the case study interview is an opportunity to showcase your critical thinking and decision-making skills. It's not uncommon for there to be multiple plausible solutions to a problem. Your ability to evaluate the pros and cons of each, weigh the trade-offs, and make a reasoned decision is what sets you apart. Supporting your decision with data or logical reasoning further strengthens your response.

Demonstrating Initiative and Leadership Skills:

The case study interview is also an excellent opportunity to demonstrate your initiative and leadership skills. Proactively leading the discussion, proposing innovative solutions, and demonstrating your willingness to take on challenges all contribute to creating a positive impression on the interviewer.

Conclusion:

In conclusion, the case study interview provides a comprehensive evaluation of your problem-solving skills, technical understanding, and business acumen, all within a practical context. Approaching it with a structured methodology, focusing on the user, and clearly articulating your thoughts will not only increase your chances of acing the interview but also provide valuable insights that will aid your career as an AI/ML product manager.

Tackling a case study interview can seem daunting, but remember, it's about more than just getting the 'right' answer. It's about demonstrating your ability to think critically, analyse complex problems, and leverage your understanding of AI/ML to propose effective and impactful solutions.

You can navigate the complexity of case study interviews through dedicated practice, understanding the varied formats, adopting a holistic perspective, maintaining logical flow, and displaying leadership skills. And in the process, you will be inching closer to acing your interview and enhancing your skills and building valuable assets for a promising career in AI/ML product management.

Chapter 14

The On-site Interview

Introduction and Purpose

Taking your first step into an on-site interview can evoke a plethora of emotions; a pulsating sense of anticipation coupled with a tinge of apprehension. This stage of the interview process is not just another hurdle to leap over but a pivotal platform to underscore your eligibility for the AI/ML product management role. It is a strenuous examination, but simultaneously, it's an exceptional chance to gain invaluable insights about your prospective company, its work environment, and its overall ethos. This discernment is crucial because compatibility with the organisation's culture can significantly impact job satisfaction, productivity, and career growth.

This on-site interview phase goes beyond verifying your professional skills; it essentially introduces you to the heartbeat of the organisation. It provides you with a sneak peek into the daily life within the company, enabling you to comprehend the business from a broader perspective. More importantly, it serves as a mirror, reflecting whether the firm's values, norms, and goals align with your own personal and professional aspirations.

Entering the on-site interview, thus, is not just about managing expectations and nervousness. It's about seizing the opportunity to shine, display your competencies, understand the organisational dynamics, and ascertain how these elements dovetail with your future ambitions.

Remember, it's not just them interviewing you, but you're also interviewing them in your quest to find the perfect fit.

Nature of the On-site Interview

The on-site interview is not merely a one-time conversation; instead, it unfolds as a series of in-depth interactions and assessments spanning a day and potentially more. This long yet enlightening journey will have you cross paths with a myriad of stakeholders who form the core teams of the organisation, such as product managers, data scientists, engineers, and even the high echelons of leadership. The purpose of this multifaceted interaction isn't just about gauging your technical know-how or testing your industry knowledge. It's a holistic examination designed to assess the breadth and depth of your competencies, behavioural attributes, and alignment with the company's culture and ethos.

Each interaction during the on-site interview has a specific objective and is meticulously designed to explore different aspects of your potential candidacy. For instance, in your discussions with other product managers, your strategic thinking, leadership qualities, and problem-solving skills might be tested. Dialogue with data scientists may steer towards understanding your grasp of AI/ML technologies and the ability to articulate their application in product development. The engineers might challenge you with hypothetical scenarios to assess your technical acumen, while senior executives could be more focused on gauging your vision for product development in alignment with the company's strategic goals.

The on-site interview hence plays an instrumental role in deciphering how well you fit into different teams and potential roles within the company. It allows the company to build a comprehensive picture of you as a potential AI/ML product manager. Can you lead a cross-functional team to a shared goal? Can you influence decision-making with your strategic insights? Can you act as an effective liaison between the technical and business sides of the organisation? Your responses and behaviour during these interactions are crucial in addressing these queries.

Moreover, this exhaustive process gives you the opportunity to observe the company's dynamics firsthand. How are the teams structured? What is the style of communication within the organisation? Is the environment collaborative or competitive? Understanding these dynamics can be insightful, helping you decide whether the company's working style resonates with yours.

Teamwork and Leadership Skills

In the complex landscape of AI/ML product management, technical skills certainly hold significant value. However, they only form part of the equation. To truly shine in the role of a product manager, and in particular, during the on-site interview, your teamwork and leadership skills are under as much scrutiny as your technical prowess. Your ability to guide and harmonise the inputs of diverse minds towards a common objective is crucial in an environment that is often characterised by the dynamic interplay of perspectives, objectives, and methodologies.

To paint a clearer picture, imagine this scenario. In a cross-functional team where you're working with engineers, data scientists, marketers, and other stakeholders, each group comes with its own set of priorities, perspectives, and methodologies. The engineers may prioritise technical feasibility; data scientists could be pushing for

the adoption of cutting-edge algorithms, while marketers might be focused on customer needs and market trends. As a product manager, you're at the centre of this multi-directional matrix. It's your role to balance these perspectives, ensure effective communication, and guide everyone towards a shared goal - a successful product that fulfils the company's strategic objectives while satisfying customer needs.

Given the centrality of these skills to the role of a product manager, on-site interviews often include exercises specifically designed to evaluate your teamwork and leadership capabilities. You may find yourself participating in group discussions or simulated tasks that test how well you can coordinate with others, negotiate between differing viewpoints, and lead a team to consensus. It's not unusual for disagreements or differences of opinion to surface during these tasks. Indeed, these moments serve as opportunities for you to demonstrate your conflict resolution skills, your capacity for empathy, and your ability to lead under pressure.

These exercises also shed light on your leadership style. Do you adopt a democratic approach, giving everyone an equal voice and seeking consensus before moving forward? Or do you lean more towards a directive style, making decisions based on your understanding and guiding the team accordingly? Each style has its merits, and the best choice often depends on the situation at hand. It's your job to demonstrate the flexibility to adopt the most effective style according to the circumstances.

Moreover, your interaction with interviewers and other candidates during the on-site interview can provide further insights into your teamwork and leadership skills. How do you conduct yourself during breaks? How do you respond to unexpected changes in the interview schedule? Your behaviour in these seemingly trivial moments can speak volumes about your ability to work and lead in a team setting.

Interviewing the Company

In the complex landscape of AI/ML product management, technical skills certainly hold significant value. However, they only form part of the equation. To truly shine in the role of a product manager, particularly during the on-site interview, your teamwork and leadership skills are under as much scrutiny as your technical prowess. Your ability to guide and harmonise the inputs of diverse minds towards a common objective is crucial in an environment that is often characterised by the dynamic interplay of perspectives, objectives, and methodologies.

To paint a clearer picture, imagine this scenario. In a cross-functional team where you're working with engineers, data scientists, marketers, and other stakeholders, each group comes with its own set of priorities, perspectives, and methodologies. The engineers may prioritise technical feasibility; data scientists could be pushing for the adoption of cutting-edge algorithms, while marketers might be focused on customer needs and market trends. As a product manager, you're at the centre of this multi-directional matrix. It's your role to balance these perspectives, ensure effective communication, and guide everyone towards a shared goal - a successful product that fulfils the company's strategic objectives while satisfying customer needs.

Given the centrality of these skills to the role of a product manager, on-site interviews often include exercises specifically designed to evaluate your teamwork and leadership capabilities. You may find yourself participating in group discussions or simulated tasks that test how well you can coordinate with others, negotiate between differing viewpoints, and lead a team to consensus. It's not unusual for disagreements or differences of opinion to surface during these tasks. Indeed, these moments serve as opportunities for you to demonstrate your conflict resolution skills, your capacity for empathy, and your ability to lead under pressure.

These exercises also shed light on your leadership style. Do you adopt a democratic approach, giving everyone an equal voice and seeking consensus before moving forward? Or do you lean more towards a directive style, making decisions based on your understanding and guiding the team accordingly? Each style has its merits, and the best choice often depends on the situation. It's your job to demonstrate the flexibility to adopt the most effective style according to the circumstances.

Moreover, your interaction with interviewers and other candidates during the on-site interview can provide further insights into your teamwork and leadership skills. How do you conduct yourself during breaks? How do you respond to unexpected changes in the interview schedule? Your behaviour in these seemingly trivial moments can speak volumes about your ability to work and lead in a team setting.

Preparing for the on-site interview is a critical task that requires thoughtful planning and strategic insight. Begin by conducting thorough research on the individuals you'll be interacting with during the interview. It's beneficial to understand their professional roles, backgrounds, and interests, as this information can help you customise your communication and responses. This research can often be as simple as a quick LinkedIn or company profile review, but its impact can be significant, allowing you to address your interviewers' specific interests and concerns.

When anticipating the expectations of various stakeholders, remember that each person will have a unique perspective on what they want in a product manager. For instance, engineers may be more interested in your technical abilities and your understanding of the development process. In contrast, a fellow product manager might focus more on your strategic planning and project management skills. Understanding these nuances allows you to prepare more effectively, shaping your responses in ways that best resonate with each interviewer.

Do not neglect the importance of practical preparation as well. If you need to present a case study or home task, ensure your laptop and slides are prepared and functioning properly. Familiarise yourself with the presentation tools, and practice your delivery to ensure a smooth, confident presentation.

On the Day of the Interview

The day of the interview brings its own set of considerations. First impressions can play a significant role in shaping the course of the interview. Present yourself professionally, both in attire and demeanour. Arriving punctually not only shows respect for the interviewer's time but also demonstrates your commitment and reliability. Start the day with an enthusiastic and open attitude. This mindset will not only help alleviate your nerves but will also convey your excitement for the role and company.

During the interview, the STAR method (Situation, Task, Action, Result) is a helpful framework for structuring your responses to behavioural questions. This method allows you to provide concrete examples, emphasising the impact of your actions and showing your ability to achieve positive outcomes.

In addition to sharing your past achievements, prepare to handle hypothetical scenarios. These are designed to assess your decision-making skills, particularly how you operate under uncertainty - a common condition in product management roles. When presented with such challenges, clearly articulate your thought process, demonstrating your ability to identify key factors, weigh options, and arrive at sound decisions.

Dealing with the Incredible

Despite thorough preparation, unexpected situations may arise during the on-site interview. You could face unexpected questions, meet individuals not initially on the interview schedule, or experience changes in the planned itinerary. While these can be disorienting, view them as opportunities to exhibit your adaptability and resourcefulness, two crucial traits for any successful product manager. Show that you can think on your feet and maintain your poise, even when the unexpected occurs.

After the Interview

Following the interview, it's important to show appreciation for the time and insights shared by each person you meet. A simple thank you note goes a long way in displaying your professionalism and courtesy. But this communication serves another purpose, too - it's an opportunity to reinforce your interest in the role and the company. Mention specific aspects of the discussion that you found particularly enlightening or interesting. This shows your attention to detail and your genuine engagement with the process.

Conclusion

In conclusion, while the on-site interview might seem like a formidable challenge, proper preparation can transform it into an empowering experience. As you walk into the company doors on the day of the interview, recall the journey that brought you to this moment. Remember the knowledge you've gained, the skills you've honed, and the preparation you've undertaken. You are ready to demonstrate your qualifications and convince them that you're the AI/ML product manager they've been searching for. Don't just aim for an offer; aim to make a lasting impact.

Your task is not merely to succeed in the interview but to emerge as an individual they can't afford to let go. So, bring your best self to the table and remember - you've got this. Good luck on your journey.

Chapter 15

Negotiating Your Offer

In the grand scheme of the interview process, negotiating your offer can often feel like the final boss battle in a gruelling video game. After demonstrating your skills and acumen in numerous rounds, you are finally at a point where the company is not just interested but ready to have you on board. However, the journey isn't over just yet. The negotiation process is your chance to ensure that you're adequately compensated for your unique set of skills and experience. It might feel uncomfortable or even confrontational, but remember; it's not just acceptable but expected for you to negotiate.

Before diving into the negotiation process, it's essential to note that your compensation should reflect your value to the company. As an AI/ML Product Manager, you're at the nexus of technological innovation and business strategy. You hold the potential to drive significant impact. This unique intersection of skills adds immense value to the company, and your compensation should reflect this.

Understanding the components of your compensation package is a good starting point. Your compensation as an AI/ML Product Manager typically includes base salary, bonus, equity, and benefits. The base salary is your fixed pay before tax. Bonus, often a percentage of your base salary, is typically tied to company and personal performance metrics. Equity represents ownership in the company and is especially relevant in startups or tech companies.

Finally, benefits include health insurance, retirement contributions, and other perks like remote work options, education stipends, and more.

Research is a crucial aspect of negotiation.
Investigate industry standards for AI/ML Product Manager roles. Use platforms like Glassdoor, LinkedIn, Payscale, and even informal discussions within your network to get a sense of what is reasonable and competitive for your role, considering your experience level and the company's size and location. This range will be your reference point during the negotiation.

When you receive the offer, express gratitude and enthusiasm about the opportunity. It's perfectly fine to ask for some time to review the details. While reviewing, consider not only the overall package but also how each component aligns with your personal priorities. For example, if the work-life balance is essential to you, flexibility in work hours or remote work options might be as crucial as the base salary.

When discussing the offer with the hiring manager or HR, be honest and transparent about your expectations. It's a conversation, not a conflict.

State your case by referring to your research and your understanding of the value you bring to the role. For example, you could say, "Given my experience in managing AI/ML products and the market rate for this role, I was expecting a base salary of X."

Don't forget to negotiate beyond salary. Consider equity, bonuses, vacation time, and other elements of the compensation package. Each of these elements can significantly affect your satisfaction with the offer.

Also, understand that every company has different pay structures and negotiation policies. Some might have rigid salary bands but can offer flexibility in bonuses or equity. Others might offer increased benefits as a means to a more competitive package.

Negotiating an offer can feel uncomfortable, but remember that this is a standard part of the process. The goal is to reach an agreement that recognizes your worth and enables you to perform your best. After all, as an AI/ML Product Manager, you're not just accepting a job, but you're also embarking on a journey that has the potential to shape the future of the company. Be confident, prepared, and forward-thinking in your approach.

This is your time to advocate for yourself, so step into the negotiation room ready to make a compelling case. And remember, regardless of the outcome, the process of negotiation is a learning experience in itself, equipping you with skills that will serve you throughout your career.

Even when a negotiation is going well, it's important not to rush. Allow yourself and the company time to digest the discussions. While negotiating can be stressful, rushing the process can lead to suboptimal decisions. Also, ensure that all aspects of your discussion are documented. Verbal agreements are good, but it's always safer to have written confirmation of any changes to your offer.

Now, let's tackle a common worry - can the offer be rescinded if you negotiate? While technically, an employer can withdraw an offer at any stage; it's generally not in their interest to do so just because a candidate negotiated. Companies expect negotiations and are usually prepared to discuss terms. It's how you negotiate that matters – being respectful and professional will always work in your favour.

Should you always negotiate? Not necessarily. If you believe the offer is fair and you're satisfied with it, it's perfectly acceptable to accept it. Sometimes, a company may put their best offer forward first, especially if they're keen on having you onboard. Trust your judgement, your research, and your understanding of the company.

Negotiation is also not just about the now. It's about your future growth within the company. Let's take equity, for example. As an AI/ML Product Manager, the products you'll develop may significantly contribute to the company's growth. In that case, having equity means you'd share in the rewards of that growth. Similarly, negotiating a clear path for progression in terms of roles and salary increases is as important as the initial package.

In all this, never lose sight of why you applied for the job in the first place. The role of an AI/ML Product Manager is a challenging yet rewarding one. The ability to shape products, influence technological advances and see tangible outcomes from your work is a unique aspect of this role. While the financial package is important, remember to factor in the non-tangible aspects - the culture of the company, the potential for learning, and the opportunity for impact.

Negotiation, in essence, is an exercise in communication and persuasion – skills that are key to a Product Manager. You need to present your case effectively and convince the other party of your viewpoint. This skill will not just land you a satisfactory offer but will also be instrumental when you step into your role. Be it influencing stakeholders or convincing your team about a product decision – the tenets are the same.

In conclusion, an offer negotiation is your opportunity to establish a relationship that is beneficial to both you and the company. Remember, you bring a unique combination of skills to the table, and the objective is to find a package that accurately reflects that. Arm yourself with thorough research, a clear understanding of your worth, and a confident attitude. Your journey as an AI/ML Product

Manager is about to begin – step into it knowing you've advocated for yourself to the best of your ability.

And finally, as you advance in your career, share your experiences and learnings. The more transparent discussions we have about job offers and negotiations, the better equipped we all will be for our own.

After all, the spirit of product management lies in constant learning and sharing of knowledge. And this book, 'From Zero to Offer: The AI & ML Product Manager's Interview Playbook,' aims to do just that – guide you, prepare you, and arm you with the information you need to navigate your AI/ML Product Manager career path. Here's to your success – from receiving that job offer to every milestone thereafter.

Part IV

Interviewing Mastery

Mastering the interviewing process is a crucial factor in progressing your career within the AI & ML industry. It is not simply about responding to questions adequately but about showcasing your skills, knowledge, and aptitude for the product manager role in a way that sets you apart from other candidates.

1. Understanding the Interviewer's Perspective

Remember, the person interviewing you is not just checking off a list of qualifications and skills. They are looking for the best fit for their team and organisation, and their assessment will be subjective and nuanced. They will consider aspects such as your communication skills, how you deal with pressure, and whether you exhibit the problem-solving capabilities critical for a PM role in AI/ML.

2. Developing a Strong Narrative

Every question is an opportunity to tell a story about your experiences and skills. Develop a compelling narrative that illustrates your unique career journey, detailing how it has led you to this point and why you are a strong candidate for the role.

3. Technical Proficiency

Technical expertise is a cornerstone for any product manager in AI/ML. Be ready to showcase your understanding of key AI/ML concepts and tools. Explain how you have used these tools to drive project success, address challenges, and generate results.

4. Demonstrating Business Acumen

Having an understanding of the wider business environment is critical. You must show that you can apply your AI/ML knowledge in a way that aligns with the company's strategy and contributes to its bottom line.

5. Showcasing Leadership and Teamwork

Product management is a role that straddles multiple teams and disciplines. Being able to work with diverse teams, lead initiatives, and manage conflicts is a necessity. Provide examples of your ability to lead and collaborate.

6. Exhibit Curiosity and Learning

The field of AI and ML is rapidly evolving. Demonstrate your ability to learn, adapt, and stay abreast of industry developments. Show your commitment to self-improvement and lifelong learning.

7. Preparing for Different Interview Formats

Be prepared for different types of interviews, such as behavioural, case study, and technical interviews. Each has its format and requires a different approach and preparation.

8. Mastering the Art of Follow-up

The process doesn't end with the interview. Follow up professionally, expressing your appreciation for the opportunity to interview and reaffirming your interest in the role.

9. Handling Rejections

Not every interview will result in a job offer. Learn to handle rejections gracefully. Seek feedback, learn from it, and use it to improve your future performance.

10. Continuous Improvement

Interviewing is a skill, and like any skill, it can be improved with practice. Always look for opportunities to hone your interviewing skills. Take every interview as a learning experience.

Remember, mastering interviews is a journey. Take it one step at a time, and don't be disheartened by the obstacles along the way. With persistence and practice, you will see progress and eventually land your desired AI/ML PM role. As you stride forward in your journey, take these tips to heart—they will surely guide your path to interviewing mastery.

Chapter 16

Common AI/ML PM Interview Questions

As your journey towards becoming an AI/ML Product Manager continues, you will inevitably face a stage that many applicants find daunting – the interview. This chapter will serve as your indispensable guide through the labyrinth of potential AI/ML PM interview questions. With meticulous preparation and a comprehensive understanding of what interviewers are seeking, you can approach this stage with well-founded confidence.

When it comes to the interview process, there are several distinct areas that the interviewers focus on: your technical understanding, your business acumen, and your soft skills. All three are crucial for a successful AI/ML Product Manager, and the blend of these skills can vary depending on the specific role and company.

Technical Understanding:

As an AI/ML Product Manager, you won't just be managing a product; you'll be managing a product powered by advanced technology. Thus, interviewers will delve into your understanding of Artificial Intelligence and Machine Learning, their workings, and their implications.

Expect questions like:

When preparing for an AI/ML product manager interview, it's crucial to anticipate the types of questions you might face. Not only does this help you feel more prepared, but it also provides an opportunity to structure your answers strategically. Here are some typical questions, along with suggested ways to respond:

- **Explain a machine learning model that you find interesting.**

This question aims to assess your understanding and interest in machine learning. A possible answer might be, "One model I find particularly fascinating is the Random Forest algorithm. What intrigues me is its versatility and accuracy in handling both regression and classification tasks. Moreover, it effectively avoids overfitting, a common issue in machine learning models, by using a multitude of decision trees and averaging their outputs.

- **How would you explain Machine Learning to a non-technical stakeholder?**

The goal here is to see if you can simplify complex ideas for a non-technical audience. A sample answer might be, "Machine Learning is akin to teaching a child how to ride a bicycle. At first, we guide the child (or the computer) by showing the correct actions. Over time, the child learns from their experiences and can ride the bike without our help. Similarly, in machine learning, we feed data to the computer and let it learn patterns, make predictions or decisions without being explicitly programmed.

- **Can you discuss a situation where you implemented an AI solution to solve a business problem?**

Interviewers ask this to understand how you have used AI to bring about real-world solutions. An answer could be, "In my previous role, we had an issue with customer churn. To tackle this, I spearheaded an AI project to develop a predictive model that analysed customer behaviour and predicted potential churn. Implementing this solution led to a 15% reduction in churn rate over the following quarter.

- **What's your strategy for dealing with resistance to AI adoption within an organisation?**

This question probes your change management skills. An appropriate response might be, "I believe in the power of education and communication. When facing resistance, I would first seek to understand the concerns driving the resistance. Then, I'd organise workshops or presentations to educate staff about AI's benefits and dispel any misconceptions. Involving everyone in the process and demonstrating quick wins can also help to win buy-in.

- **What are some ethical considerations when implementing AI/ML technologies?**

Ethics in AI is a significant concern. A possible answer might be, "Some ethical considerations include data privacy, bias in AI models, and job displacement due to AI automation. As a product manager, it's crucial to work with legal, HR, and data teams to ensure we address these issues and maintain transparency with users about how we use AI."

- **Describe a time when you had to prioritise one feature over another. How did you make that decision?**

This question tests your decision-making skills. You could say, "In a previous project, I had to choose between enhancing our product's user interface and adding a new feature. Although both were important, I prioritised the new feature because user feedback indicated it was a critical need. It was a tough decision, but we managed to deliver value to our users, which led to a significant increase in user engagement.

- **How do you keep up with the latest trends in AI/ML?**

This question gauges your commitment to continuous learning. An answer could be, "I keep myself updated by reading AI research papers, following relevant blogs and podcasts, and participating in AI communities and forums. I also regularly attend AI-related conferences and webinars."

- **Describe a time you had to make a difficult decision with limited data**.

This question examines how you operate in uncertain situations. A possible response might be, "In my last role, we had to decide whether to launch a product feature without having much data about its potential success. I led a team that brainstormed potential scenarios, assessed risks and made a contingency plan. Eventually, we decided to go ahead, and the feature was well-received."

- **How would you measure the success of an AI feature you've launched?**

The question assesses your understanding of performance metrics. An answer might be, "Success can be measured using various metrics, depending on the feature's goals. These might include user engagement, the accuracy of the AI model, reduced manual effort, or increased sales. It's also crucial to consider qualitative feedback from users."

- **What's your approach to managing the different stakeholders involved in an AI project?**

This question is about your stakeholder management skills. An appropriate answer could be, "I believe in regular and clear communication. It's important to understand each stakeholder's needs and expectations and ensure that everyone is aligned on the project goals and timeline. Regular updates and involving stakeholders in decision-making helps keep everyone engaged and minimises surprises."

Remember, the aim is not only to demonstrate your knowledge of AI/ML but also to show how you can apply these concepts in real-life scenarios to add value. Prepare, practice, and present your ideas clearly, and you'll increase your chances of success in your AI/ML product management interview.

Through such questions, interviewers aim to discern your grasp of the technology you'll be dealing with. It's not just about having bookish knowledge; you need to demonstrate how you've applied or how you would apply these concepts in real-world scenarios.

Business Acumen:

Being a Product Manager in the field of Artificial Intelligence and Machine Learning (AI/ML) goes beyond purely technical know-how. One of the vital roles of a PM is to strategically navigate the product through the intricate matrix of business operations. Hence, having strong business acumen is essential in the world of product management.

The term 'business acumen' refers to the ability to comprehend and cope with various aspects of a business simultaneously, make sound decisions, and produce the best possible results. In an AI/ML environment, business acumen acts as the bridge between sophisticated technology and the tangible benefits it can provide to the business.

Firstly, designing a product that aligns with the business goals is fundamental. As an AI/ML product manager, you will need to understand the company's strategic objectives and ensure the product you're developing or managing contributes effectively to those objectives. This might involve anything from improving operational efficiency to opening up new revenue streams or enhancing customer satisfaction.

Next, the capacity to anticipate market trends is an essential part of the job. In the rapidly evolving AI/ML landscape, new technologies, applications, and competitors are continually emerging. A successful product manager keeps their finger on the pulse of these changes, adjusting the product strategy as needed to keep it competitive and innovative.

Understanding customer requirements is another crucial element of business acumen. You need to have a deep comprehension of who your customers are, what they want, and how they behave. In the world of AI/ML, this could involve everything from analysing usage data to conducting customer interviews or surveys. By putting the customer at the centre of your product strategy, you can ensure that your product meets their needs and solves their problems.

Furthermore, a product manager must have a vision for the product. In an AI/ML context, this means being able to see how the technology can evolve and continue to add value in the future. It's about painting a compelling picture of the product's future - one that motivates the team, excites customers and convinces stakeholders. This vision will serve as a guiding star, informing your strategy and decision-making.

Finally, the ability to interpret and use financial information is a critical aspect of business acumen. As a product manager, you'll be involved in budgeting, forecasting, and financial planning for your product. Understanding key financial metrics can help you make better decisions and demonstrate the financial viability and impact of your product to stakeholders.

Typical questions include:

The role of an AI/ML Product Manager is dynamic and complex. As such, the interview process often includes questions designed to test your ability to think strategically, make decisions, and understand the product lifecycle in its entirety. These questions will challenge your problem-solving skills, commercial awareness, and leadership abilities, so prepare to share specific examples from your past experiences that highlight these strengths.

- **Can you describe a situation where you had to make a significant strategic decision that impacted the direction of a product?**

This question assesses your decision-making abilities under pressure. An ideal response could highlight a time when you faced a challenging situation and made a strategic decision that positively influenced the product's direction. Discuss the factors you considered, the steps you took to evaluate options, and how you communicated and implemented your decision.

- **How would you approach a scenario where a critical feature in your product roadmap was not well-received by customers?**

Interviewers are interested in your ability to adapt your strategy based on customer feedback. A good response might involve outlining your approach to collecting and analysing customer feedback, iterating the product, and working with your team to address the concerns raised.

- **Describe a situation when you had to prioritise a feature due to resource constraints.**

This question seeks to understand your ability to make tough choices and prioritise effectively. Share an example that demonstrates your ability to consider multiple factors, such as business objectives, customer needs, and resource availability, when making decisions.

- **How do you approach competitor analysis, and can you share an instance when such analysis influenced your product decisions?**

With this question, interviewers assess your understanding of the competitive landscape and its implications on product strategy. Detail your process for conducting a competitor analysis and give an example of when such an analysis directly influenced your product's features, positioning, or marketing strategy.

- **How do you measure the success of a product or a feature post-launch?**

This question gauges your understanding of key performance indicators and metrics used in product management. Explain how you set objectives and key results (OKRs) and how you leverage data to measure success.

- **Tell us about a time when you had to convince a stakeholder who disagreed with your product decision.**

This question probes your interpersonal and negotiation skills. Discuss a time when you had to stand by your product decision, how you presented your case, and how you resolved the disagreement while maintaining a good relationship with the stakeholder.

- **Describe a time when a product you managed failed to meet expectations. How did you handle it?**

Interviewers use this question to understand your resilience and problem-solving skills. Share an instance when things didn't go as planned, how you dealt with the situation, and what you learned from the experience.

- **How do you ensure your team stays aligned with the product vision?**

This question assesses your leadership and communication skills. Describe your approach to communicating the product vision to your team and keeping them engaged and motivated to achieve it.

- **Can you discuss a time when you identified a market opportunity for your product?**

This question is designed to examine your strategic thinking and market awareness. Discuss a time when you spotted an opportunity in the market, how you validated it, and the impact it had on your product.

- **Describe a situation where you had to make a critical decision about a product without all the necessary information.**

Interviewers ask this question to gauge your decision-making skills under uncertainty. Share an instance where you had to make a decision despite incomplete data, outlining how you assessed the situation, evaluated risks, and arrived at your decision.

These questions can offer valuable insights into your capabilities as an AI/ML product manager. By providing clear, concise, and context-rich responses, you can demonstrate.

The Importance of Soft Skills in Product Management:

Product management is a multidimensional role that requires a delicate balance of technical knowledge, business acumen, and, equally important, soft skills. These are the personal attributes that enable an individual to interact effectively and harmoniously with others, fostering productive and positive relationships. As a Product Manager, you often serve as a conduit between various teams, including developers, marketers, salespeople, and customers. Therefore, possessing strong communication skills, leadership abilities, and a knack for team collaboration is not just desirable but essential.

Soft skills, contrary to what the term may suggest, are not easy to master, but they are the glue that holds the multifaceted role of a product manager together. They help forge connections, build trust, and ensure alignment of goals across diverse groups, each speaking their own language of expertise. The soft skills of a Product Manager extend beyond mere language proficiency; they encompass empathy, the ability to inspire, conflict resolution, and a capacity for active listening.

Communication, for instance, is not simply about sharing information but ensuring that the intended message is understood, accepted, and acted upon. It is about the art of storytelling, of painting a clear picture of the product vision, and inspiring others to join you on the journey towards that vision. An effective communicator can translate complex technical jargon into plain-spoken language, enabling non-technical stakeholders to understand the product's features and value proposition.

Similarly, leadership is not about issuing directives or being at the helm of decision-making. It's about empowering teams, fostering a culture of innovation, and guiding them towards achieving common objectives. A great leader recognises the unique strengths of each team member, creating an environment where everyone feels valued and heard. They take responsibility for their team's successes and failures, providing constructive feedback and celebrating achievements along the way.

Collaboration, another key soft skill, is at the heart of product management. It involves breaking down silos, encouraging cross-functional teamwork, and fostering a shared sense of ownership over the product. An effective collaborator understands the importance of diversity, appreciating that the best ideas often emerge from the confluence of different perspectives. They value each team member's input, bridging gaps between departments and ensuring that everyone is moving in the same direction.

Negotiation and persuasion are also crucial soft skills for a product manager. With various stakeholders to manage, each with their priorities and objectives, conflicts and disagreements are inevitable. A good product manager can navigate these challenging scenarios, leveraging their negotiation skills to find mutually beneficial solutions while maintaining positive relationships. This ability to persuade and influence helps secure buy-in from stakeholders, which is critical for driving the product vision forward.

The importance of **emotional intelligence** cannot be understated. It is about being attuned to your emotions and those of others, using this understanding to manage behaviour and relationships effectively. Emotional intelligence is a key driver of effective leadership and teamwork. It allows product managers to empathise with customers, understand team dynamics, and lead with compassion and understanding.

In essence, soft skills are the lubricants that keep the machinery of product management running smoothly. They foster a culture of understanding, mutual respect, and unity within teams, ensuring that everyone works towards the same goal despite their diverse backgrounds and areas of expertise. They help to resolve conflicts, drive collaboration, and ensure effective communication, promoting an environment of productivity and positive engagement. By honing these soft skills, a Product

Common questions that aim to evaluate these skills are:

Evaluating Soft Skills Through Common Interview Questions

Product management involves a significant degree of people management, which is why an understanding and demonstration of soft skills are so crucial. Evaluating these skills often involves asking behavioural questions that delve into your past experiences. Below are ten questions that are commonly asked, alongside a summary of what a compelling response might include:

- **Can you give an example of a time when you led a team through a difficult project or situation?**

This question is designed to gauge your leadership skills and resilience. An ideal response would detail a challenging situation, your approach to leading the team, how you managed stress, and the final outcome.

- **How do you ensure clear and effective communication within your team?**

This question seeks to evaluate your communication skills. A great answer might describe your strategies for maintaining open lines of communication, such as regular meetings, clear and concise emails, or leveraging communication tools.

- **Tell me about a time when you had to adapt your communication style to suit a particular audience.**

This question assesses your ability to tailor your communication to different stakeholders. Your response could involve a scenario where you had to simplify complex technical terms for non-technical stakeholders or adjust your communication style to suit a different culture or work environment.

- **How have you used your emotional intelligence in a professional setting?**

Interviewers ask this to understand your emotional awareness and empathy. You could describe a situation where you recognised a team member's emotional state and adjusted your actions accordingly, leading to a positive outcome.

- **Describe a situation where you had to manage a conflict between two team members**

This question tests your conflict resolution skills. Detail a scenario where you had to mediate a disagreement, ensuring you highlight the steps you took to understand both perspectives and reach a mutually agreeable resolution.

- **Can you share an instance where your adaptability was tested during a project?**

This question probes your flexibility and ability to deal with change. Share a story where unforeseen changes affected your project and how you adapted your strategies to deal with these changes effectively.

- **How do you handle stress and maintain productivity in high-pressure situations?**

Interviewers ask this to understand your stress management strategies. Describe techniques you use to maintain calm and productivity under pressure, such as prioritisation, delegation, mindfulness, or seeking support when necessary.

- **Describe a time when you had to influence a stakeholder who was resistant to your ideas.**

This question gauges your negotiation and persuasion skills. Share a scenario where you faced resistance from a stakeholder and how you managed to convince them to see things from your perspective.

- **How do you encourage collaboration within a cross-functional team?**

This question aims to assess your team collaboration skills. Discuss strategies you've employed to foster a collaborative spirit within a diverse team, such as team-building activities, open discussions, or shared goals.

- **Can you discuss a situation where you had to balance your team's needs with the company's objectives?**

This question probes your ability to balance different priorities. Share an instance where you had to consider your team's capacity or preferences alongside the company's objectives and how you managed to strike a balance.

Remember, when answering these questions, it's crucial to use the STAR method (Situation, Task, Action, Result). This approach allows you to provide clear, structured, and comprehensive responses that effectively showcase your soft skills in action. By doing so, you can demonstrate your ability to effectively manage not just products but people and relationships as well, which are vital aspects of the product management role.

Assessing Innovation and Creativity in Interviews

Innovation and creativity play a pivotal role in the dynamic field of AI/ML product management. Employers are increasingly seeking individuals who possess not just technical knowledge but also an imaginative vision to push boundaries and drive the product towards unexplored horizons.

Below, we've presented ten interview questions, along with exemplar answers, that aim to probe your innovative and creative capabilities.

- **What emerging trends in AI/ML do you think could be leveraged to enhance our product?**

This question seeks to test your awareness of industry trends and your ability to apply them innovatively. Your answer could discuss a recent AI/ML advancement like federated learning or reinforcement learning and elaborate on how this could enhance the company's product or service.

- **Describe an AI/ML project you've worked on that required a high level of innovation**

With this question, interviewers want to know about your innovative experiences. You could discuss a project where you implemented a novel AI/ML algorithm or developed a unique model to solve a challenging problem.

- **How would you encourage innovation within your team?**

Here, the focus is on your leadership in fostering creativity and innovation. You might discuss strategies like brainstorming sessions, hackathons, promoting a fail-fast-learn-quickly culture, or giving recognition for innovative ideas.

- **Tell me about a time when you took a calculated risk in a project to achieve a better outcome**

This question probes your risk-taking aptitude for innovation. An ideal answer could share a scenario where you adopted a less-travelled approach or used an unconventional technique that ultimately paid off.

- **If you could add one revolutionary feature to our product that would set us apart from our competitors, what would it be?**

This question tests your creative thinking and understanding of the product. Here, you can suggest a forward-thinking feature that would provide significant value to users and distinguish the product in the market.

- **How do you validate or test the potential of a new, innovative idea?**

This question seeks to understand your process of vetting innovative ideas. You might talk about performing a SWOT analysis, conducting user research, or utilising an MVP (Minimum Viable Product) approach.

1. **How would you foster a culture of continuous learning and upskilling in your team to keep up with AI/ML advancements?**

Interviewers ask this to assess your commitment to continuous learning. Discuss strategies such as regular workshops, attending conferences, facilitating knowledge-sharing sessions, or providing resources for self-learning.

- **Tell me about a time when you had to think outside of the box to solve a complex problem**

This question seeks to understand your creative problem-solving skills. Highlight a situation where traditional solutions were ineffective, and you had to devise an unconventional solution.

- **Can you describe an instance where your innovative idea failed? How did you learn from it?**

This question tests your ability to learn from failures. Share an instance where your innovative solution didn't work as expected, and discuss the learning experience and how it helped you grow.

- **How would you utilise AI/ML to improve customer experience?**

The focus here is on your customer-centric innovation. Suggest how specific AI/ML technologies (like chatbots, personalised recommendations, and predictive analytics) could enhance customer experience.
  - When responding to these questions, it's crucial to not just describe your innovative ideas but also explain the thought processes and actions that led to

their inception and execution. Demonstrating this mindset in the interview can effectively show that you possess the creative acuity and innovative drive that is so vital in the ever-evolving field of AI/ML product management.

Evaluating Ethics and Responsibility in Interviews

Ethical considerations and social responsibilities are now fundamental aspects of AI/ML technologies. With their growing impact on society, AI/ML product managers must navigate these issues with integrity and a deep understanding of ethical principles. In the following, we will delve into ten interview questions and sample responses that probe your

comprehension and approach towards ethical implications in AI/ML.

- **Describe a scenario in which you had to make an ethical decision regarding data privacy**

  With this question, the interviewer seeks to understand your sensitivity towards data privacy, a crucial ethical concern in AI/ML. You might discuss a situation where you had to balance data utilisation for AI model improvement against preserving user privacy.

- **What are some potential risks and ethical implications of AI-powered recommendation systems?** This question tests your awareness of potential pitfalls in AI/ML systems. You could address issues like echo chambers, misinformation spread, or potential bias in recommendations.

- **How would you ensure transparency in the AI products you manage?** Transparency in AI is crucial for user trust. Your answer could cover strategies such as implementing explainable AI, transparent data policies, or user-friendly reporting of AI decisions.

- **Tell me about a time when you had to advocate for an ethical stance in your team?** This question aims to understand your commitment to ethics even in challenging situations. You could share an instance where you stood up against a potentially harmful application of AI/ML or unethical data usage.

- **How would you approach developing an AI system that needs to make decisions affecting human lives, such as in healthcare or autonomous vehicles?** This question explores your approach to ethical decision-making in critical applications of AI. You could address the importance of rigorous testing, transparency, compliance with regulatory standards, and the inclusion of human oversight.

- **What measures would you take to prevent or mitigate algorithmic bias?** Algorithmic bias is a significant concern in AI/ML. Discuss techniques like balanced training data, robust testing for bias, transparency in algorithmic decision-making, and continuous monitoring for biased outcomes.

- **How would you communicate to customers about the use of AI in our products?** This question tests your ability to communicate transparently about AI with users. Discuss the importance of clear communication about how user data is used, how decisions are made, and how users can control their data.

- **If you discovered an unethical practice in your team, such as misuse of user data, how would you handle it?** This question assesses your integrity and willingness to uphold ethical standards. Explain the importance of addressing the issue directly, escalating it to higher management if necessary, and ensuring remedial actions are taken.

- **What is your approach to the ethical implications of AI/ML in regard to job displacement?** This question probes your understanding of the wider societal implications of AI/ML. You could discuss strategies for managing this impact, such as supporting re-skilling initiatives and promoting AI as a tool to assist rather than replace human jobs.

- **How would you ensure that the AI/ML products you manage comply with various global data protection regulations?** Compliance with data regulations is a key ethical responsibility in AI/ML. Discuss strategies such as keeping abreast with global data protection regulations, involving legal experts, and implementing robust data governance practices.

Providing thoughtful and considerate responses to these questions can help you demonstrate your understanding and commitment towards ethical considerations in AI/ML. As an AI/ML product manager, embodying ethical values and principles is crucial for maintaining social trust in the technology and for the long-term sustainability and success of your product.

Understanding Adaptability in AI/ML Interviews

The dynamic and fast-paced nature of AI/ML demands product managers that are adaptable and flexible. Your capacity to learn new technologies, adopt novel approaches, and pivot in response to industry changes is essential. Below are ten potential interview questions, along with sample answers, that demonstrate your adaptability in this ever-evolving field.

- **How have you incorporated new AI/ML tools or frameworks into your product development process?** This question allows you to discuss instances where you've effectively implemented new technological tools or methodologies, showcasing your ability to stay abreast with innovations in the field.

- **Tell me about a time when a product feature you were developing became obsolete before launch. How did you respond?** In this scenario, you might describe how you quickly shifted gears, worked with your team to develop a more relevant feature, and learned from the experience to prevent similar occurrences in the future.

- **How would you handle a situation where a critical team member leaves in the middle of a project?** This question tests your adaptability in human resource crises. Your answer could involve finding a temporary solution, effectively redistributing the workload, and recruiting a suitable replacement.

- **Discuss a time when you had to adapt your product due to changes in market trends.** You could talk about a time when you noticed a shift in the market trend and quickly adapted your product strategy to cater to the new demand, illustrating your ability to stay attuned to market dynamics.

- **Can you recall a situation where a change in company strategy required you to reevaluate your product's direction?** Here, share an example of when you successfully navigated a major strategic shift, demonstrating your capacity to adapt to broader business changes.

- **How would you approach a situation where a trusted AI/ML model fails to perform as expected?** In response, you could discuss your problem-solving approach, focusing on your adaptability in troubleshooting and refining the model or transitioning to a more suitable one.

- **Tell me about a time when a stakeholder's feedback significantly altered your product roadmap.** This question invites you to share a scenario where you demonstrated flexibility and adaptability to incorporate valuable feedback, even if it required substantial changes.

- **How do you keep yourself updated with the latest trends in AI/ML?** This question allows you to highlight resources or practices you engage with to stay current, showcasing your proactive learning habits.

- **Discuss an instance where you had to pivot your product to comply with new regulations.** This query helps you exhibit your ability to swiftly adapt to legal changes, underlining your understanding of the regulatory landscape in AI/ML.

- **Describe a scenario where you had to make decisions with incomplete information**. Here, you can share an instance where you took calculated risks, balancing your actions between available information and intuitive judgement.

Your ability to adapt in the face of change is vital as an AI/ML product manager. By answering these questions effectively, you can demonstrate your resilience, flexibility, and commitment to continuous learning, which are highly valued traits in this dynamic field. In answering these questions, your aim should be to showcase your ability to navigate team dynamics, maintain open communication, and foster a positive working environment.

In essence, the interview for an AI/ML Product Manager position is a test of your technical prowess, your business sensibility, and your people management skills. It's a tall order, no doubt, but that's what makes this role so challenging and exciting. As you prepare for your interview, remember that the aim is not just to provide textbook answers but to demonstrate how your unique blend of skills makes you the perfect fit for the role. Take the time to reflect on your experiences and how they've shaped you as a professional.

As we progress further into this exciting journey, remember that the 'From Zero to Offer: The AI & ML Product Manager's Interview Playbook' is here to guide you every step of the way.

In conclusion, an AI/ML PM interview is a multidimensional evaluation of your technical understanding, business acumen, people management skills, creativity, ethical considerations, and adaptability. Remember, every question is an opportunity to demonstrate how your unique blend of these skills makes you a compelling candidate for the role.

Although it might seem intimidating, consider the interview as a conversation where you learn as much about the company and role as they learn about you. This two-way exchange will help you make an informed decision about whether the role aligns with your career goals and values.

Now, armed with this chapter's insights, you are better equipped to tackle the gamut of questions that will come your way in an AI/ML PM interview. The next chapter will delve into more specific and complex AI/ML PM interview scenarios to further prepare you for success.

Keep in mind that the journey to becoming an AI/ML Product Manager is not a sprint but a marathon. It requires persistent effort, continuous learning, and unwavering dedication. Yet, the rewards of this journey – playing a part in shaping the future of technology – are unquestionably worth the effort.

Stay curious, remain eager to learn, and keep striving towards your goal. This book, **'From Zero to Offer: The AI & ML Product Manager's** Interview Playbook', will continue to be your guiding light on this exciting journey. The journey from zero to offer starts now!

Chapter 17

Post-Interview Tips

After the adrenaline and anticipation of an AI/ML Product Manager interview subsides, candidates often find themselves in a mixed emotional state, oscillating between relief and anxiety. Exiting the interview room doesn't mean your endeavour has ended; it signifies the beginning of a crucial phase that demands strategic navigation.

The post-interview period is a strategic zone of its own, often underestimated in importance. It is not merely a waiting game but an opportunity to reinforce your interest, clarify lingering doubts, and maintain a line of communication with the potential employer. This chapter offers insights on managing this stage with tact, thereby maintaining a favourable impression and increasing your chances of landing the job.

Firstly, it's essential to debrief yourself after the interview. Reflect on the discussion, noting key points, impressions, and any room for improvement. This personal feedback is invaluable, providing learning points for future interviews and offering a benchmark for your own progress.

A well-crafted thank-you note can go a long way in maintaining a positive impression. Dispatch an appreciative message within 24 hours, thanking your interviewer for their time and highlighting aspects of the interview or the company that you found particularly engaging. This serves a dual purpose - it not only reminds the interviewer of your keen interest but also provides an opportunity to subtly reinforce why you would be a good fit for the role.

Follow-ups are an integral part of post-interview etiquette. However, maintaining a delicate balance is important; you want to display your interest without appearing desperate or impatient. If you haven't heard back after the time they mentioned for feedback, it is perfectly acceptable to send a polite follow-up email.

This period is also an opportunity to evaluate the company from your perspective. Was the interview process organised and respectful? Did you feel valued? Your observations can offer insights into the company's culture and how they treat their employees.

Furthermore, continue with your job search and interview preparations. This period of uncertainty shouldn't halt your progress. Instead, utilise this time to hone your skills further, keep abreast with industry trends, and explore other potential opportunities.

Lastly, be patient. Decisions about job offers can take time as companies often have internal procedures to follow. Remember, the post-interview phase is a test of your patience, resilience, and positive outlook as much as the interview itself. Approach this phase with the same professionalism and determination that you brought to your interview, and you'll navigate it successfully.

Reflect on the Interview

Take time to reflect on your performance while your memories of the interview are still fresh. What went well? What could you have improved? Were there any questions that stumped you? Reflecting on these points can provide valuable insights for future interviews.

Send a Follow-up Thank You Note

An often underutilised strategy is sending a thank you note to the interviewer. This simple gesture can go a long way in showing your professionalism and continued interest in the role. Be sure to keep it brief, personalised and sincere. A hastily written, generic thank you note might do more harm than good, so put some thought into it.

Keep Up with the Market

Don't slack off on your market research, and stay abreast of the latest developments in AI/ML. If you're waiting to hear back from one company, remember that this doesn't prevent you from continuing to look for other opportunities. You should always be ready to grab new opportunities or face more interviews.

Reconnect with your Network

Now is a good time to reconnect with your network. Let them know how your interview went and what you learned. They might provide you with additional insights or connect you with new opportunities. Plus, they'll appreciate hearing from you and strengthening your professional relationships.

Stay Positive and Patient

Waiting for a response post-interview can be nerve-wracking. It's easy to overthink things and jump to conclusions. Stay positive, and keep in mind that hiring processes often take longer than expected.

Handle Rejection Professionally

If you're not selected, remember that rejection is a part of life and, more importantly, a part of the job search process. Handle it professionally. Reply with a polite and gracious message, thanking them for their time and consideration. Ask for feedback if it feels appropriate and use this as a learning opportunity for future interviews.

Interview Debrief

If the company doesn't provide feedback, do a self-debrief.

Consider asking a trusted mentor, friend, or family member to replay some of the questions you remember from the interview. They can provide a fresh perspective on your responses.

Preparation for the Next Steps

Success in the initial interview stage for an AI/ML Product Manager position, while commendable, is only the commencement of a broader journey. Your persistence and diligence in preparing for each stage of the recruitment process can make the difference between a good candidate and a great one. It's crucial, therefore, not to become complacent but to consider every positive step forward as motivation to excel further.

Receiving positive feedback from your interview should be seen as a springboard towards comprehensive preparation for the subsequent phases. This is a time to capitalise on your initial success and build on the foundation you've already established. The continuity and depth of your preparation could be the differentiating factor in the final hiring decision.

Consider refining your understanding of the company. While initial research would have given you a broad overview, deepening your knowledge about the organisation's business model, culture, strategic goals, and challenges can give you an edge. Explore recent news articles, quarterly reports, and industry analyses to glean more intricate details about the company and its market position.

Simultaneously, keep an eye on the broader industry landscape. Developments in AI/ML technologies are rapid, and staying informed of the latest trends and advancements can showcase your industry engagement and passion for the field. Engaging in webinars, attending relevant conferences, and subscribing to industry publications could offer you timely insights and inspire innovative ideas.

Constructively using the information from the initial interview can also contribute significantly to your preparation for the next steps. Reflect upon the information you have gathered about the role, the team, and the company's expectations. Consider the queries and discussions that took place in the first meeting, as these can provide key insights into the areas of focus for the subsequent rounds.

Another vital element of preparation involves crafting meaningful questions for the next round of interviews.

Thoughtful, well-researched questions can demonstrate your analytical abilities, your curiosity, and your serious interest in the role and the company. Try to develop questions that provoke insightful conversations about the company's strategy, the role of AI/ML within the organisation, and the team's aspirations and challenges.

The Art of Negotiation: Balancing Worth and Market Standards

Congratulations!

If you've reached the negotiation stage, you've successfully navigated through the rigorous selection process for an AI/ML Product Manager role. However, the final step—negotiation—requires a careful, considerate approach. This phase is about more than just your salary; it is a nuanced conversation that encompasses all aspects of your potential employment.

Negotiation can sometimes feel uncomfortable or confrontational, but it need not be. It's important to remember that this is a normal part of the recruitment process, and your future employer expects you to engage in this conversation. This dialogue is about aligning your personal value with the company's valuation of your worth and striking a balance between the two.

One of the key components to successful negotiation is preparation. You should have a clear understanding of your value proposition as an AI/ML product manager, which you've articulated and demonstrated throughout the interview process. Also, you should have a deep understanding of the industry's standard compensation packages for similar roles. Salary survey sites, recruitment firms, and industry peers can be excellent sources of this information. Armed with these insights, you can enter the negotiation process with a clear sense of your worth and realistic expectations.

Approach the conversation with an open mind, being respectful and reasonable. Remember, the goal is to arrive at a win-win solution that satisfies both your needs and those of the company. Express your expectations clearly, providing a rationale that supports your stance.

Salary is often the most focused-upon aspect of negotiation, but it's not the only element up for discussion. You can also negotiate benefits, flexible working hours, professional development opportunities, vacation time, stock options, and sometimes even your job title or role specifics. These aspects can significantly influence your job satisfaction and career progression.

Remember to listen and show empathy. Understand that there are budget constraints and organisational policies that the company needs to consider. If the company can't meet your salary expectation, explore if there are other benefits or opportunities they can offer that would be of value to you.

One key aspect of negotiation that is often overlooked is the timing. It's best to discuss details when you have a written job offer in hand. It is at this point that you have the maximum leverage since the company has shown a firm interest in hiring you.

Lastly, it's crucial to remember that while negotiation is important, the goal is not to 'win' but to establish a positive, respectful professional relationship that sets the foundation for your tenure at the company. Negotiating successfully is about maintaining a balance between asserting your worth and understanding the market standards, leading to an agreement that both parties are pleased with.

Remember, the interview process doesn't end once you've finished answering the questions. The actions you take after the interview can have a significant impact on your chances of success. Following the strategies above can help you leave a lasting impression, improve for future interviews, and ultimately increase your chances of receiving a job offer.

From Reflection to Action: Maximising the Post-Interview Phase

The period following an AI/ML Product Manager interview is like a blank canvas—a space brimming with opportunities for reflection, learning, growth, and strategic planning. Regardless of the interview's outcome, the steps you take during this critical period can sharpen your competitive edge, strengthen your professional networks, and significantly boost your chances of securing your ideal role.

Soliciting Feedback: The Mirror to Your Performance

Whether you've clinched the job or not, the pursuit of constructive feedback post-interview is a move that pays dividends. It's a unique opportunity to glean insights from an insider's perspective about your strengths and areas of improvement. It's as if you're being granted a looking glass into how you were perceived by the very people who were deliberating over your fit for the role.

Remember to ask for feedback politely and professionally. This could be in your follow-up email, where you thank the interviewers for their time and the opportunity to learn more about the company. A simple request for any observations on your performance or areas you could work on is usually received positively and can provide invaluable guidance for future interviews.

Stay Organised: Your Future Self Will Thank You

The organisation is paramount in a job search. Documenting details about the companies and roles you've interviewed for, including specifics about the interview process itself, can serve as a vital personal database. This could encompass the names of your interviewers, any challenging questions you grappled with, responses you felt resonated well, and an overall evaluation of your performance. This repository of information becomes especially beneficial if you're managing multiple interviews, providing you with a quick reference for each company's distinct interview landscape.

Your Professional Avatar: Active Presence on Social Media

An engaged presence on professional social media platforms such as LinkedIn is increasingly becoming a marker of a proactive professional. Regularly sharing pertinent industry news, commenting thoughtfully on posts by other professionals in your field, and joining relevant discussions can boost your visibility. It keeps you updated with the latest trends, cultivates a community of like-minded professionals, and could make you more attractive to potential employers who appreciate an active and informed candidate.

Cultivating a Growth Mindset: Continuous Learning

Reflecting on your interview performance might highlight areas where your knowledge could be deepened or skills polished. The interim period, while you await the interview result, is a valuable window to address these gaps. The pursuit of continuous learning exemplifies your commitment to your professional development, making you a more compelling candidate for future AI/ML PM roles. This could involve taking an online course, attending webinars, or reading up on relevant topics.

Strategic Planning: Preparing for the Next Horizon

Irrespective of this interview's outcome, you need to gear up for what's next. What other companies align with your aspirations? Which roles are a match for your skills and experience? Start charting your trajectory, consider other roles, and even kickstart the application process. Maintain your momentum, ensuring that you're not entirely reliant on one opportunity.

Well-being: Self-care Isn't Selfish

Interviews can be taxing, and the anticipation of the outcome even more so. It's essential to recognise the need for self-care during this period. Ensuring your mental and physical well-being should be a top priority. This could involve regular exercise, meditation, delving into a good book, or any activity that helps you unwind and rejuvenate.

The post-interview phase of your AI/ML Product Manager journey should be seen as an empowering process. It's a chance to reflect, enhance your professional persona, build strong networks, and prepare for future opportunities. Approach this period with a positive and proactive mindset, remembering that every interview, irrespective of its result, is a stepping-stone that moves you closer to your goal.

Part V

Succeeding and Advancing in Your AI/ML Product Manager Career

While navigating the AI/ML product management terrain and successfully securing a position is an accomplishment in itself, it's only the start of your career journey. The road ahead necessitates continual growth, consistent performance, and an aptitude for adaptability. In this chapter, we'll delve into strategies to aid you in succeeding and propelling your career as an AI/ML Product Manager.

1. Embrace Lifelong Learning

In the fast-paced, ever-evolving world of AI and ML, the ability to adapt and learn continuously is paramount. Stay attuned to the latest industry advancements, technological innovations, and trends. Attend webinars, seminars, and conferences; pursue relevant certifications and courses; engage in self-study; and subscribe to AI/ML publications and blogs.

2. Nurture a Product Mindset

A successful AI/ML PM must comprehend the product lifecycle intricately, making data-driven decisions, define clear product goals, and identifying unique value propositions. Building and nurturing a product mindset, therefore, is an essential component of career advancement.

3. Foster Technical Acumen

While it's not expected of you to code, a solid understanding of AI/ML technologies, their applications, limitations, and underlying principles is crucial. Technical proficiency will aid in bridging the gap between the technical and non-technical teams, resulting in a more harmonious and effective working environment.

4. Cultivate Leadership Skills

The role of an AI/ML PM often entails leading cross-functional teams. Developing your leadership skills - from communication and conflict resolution to empathy and delegation - is pivotal. Additionally, demonstrating thought leadership in AI/ML by publishing articles, speaking at conferences, or being actively involved in professional communities can enhance your career progression.

5. Develop Strong Stakeholder Management Skills

An AI/ML PM must navigate a plethora of stakeholders - from engineers and data scientists to business leaders and clients. Possessing the skills to manage expectations, communicate effectively, and negotiate is vital.

6. Advocate for Ethical AI Practices

The ethical implications of AI/ML are an increasingly prominent conversation. As an AI/ML PM, you have a responsibility to advocate for ethical AI practices. This means ensuring transparency, fairness, and privacy in AI systems and avoiding bias in AI/ML models and applications.

7. Excel at Project Management

Delivering successful AI/ML products requires exquisite project management. Proficiency in Agile, Scrum, or other project management methodologies can ensure efficient execution of the product development lifecycle.

8. Strive for Impact

Above all, focus on the impact of your work. From improving the user experience and driving revenue growth to advance AI/ML applications for societal good, strive to deliver products that make a difference.

9. Plan for Your Career Progression

Think about your long-term career goals. Whether advancing to a senior PM role, transitioning into a different role within AI/ML, or launching your own AI startup, having a clear vision will guide your decisions and actions.

10. Care for Your Well-being

The rigorous demands of an AI/ML PM role can be challenging. It's essential to prioritise your mental and physical well-being. Develop a routine that fosters work-life balance, including regular exercise, healthy eating, and time for relaxation and hobbies.

Securing the job offer is merely the first step. To truly excel and advance in your career as an AI/ML PM, you must commit to continual learning, exhibit leadership, be technically proficient, and understand the product lifecycle intricately. But, most importantly, remember to measure success not only by professional achievements but also by personal growth and well-being. With these strategies in mind you are well-positioned to build a rewarding and successful career in AI/ML product management.

11. Master the Art of Communication

As an AI/ML PM, you are expected to act as the conduit between various teams. Your success will depend on how well you translate complex technical details into actionable insights for stakeholders. To do so effectively, hone your communication skills – both written and verbal.

12. Understanding User Needs

Understanding user needs and translating them into product features is a crucial skill for any product manager. This becomes even more important in AI/ML products due to the intricacy and complexity of these technologies. Regular user research, analytics, and a deep understanding of your market are key.

13. Master the Business Side

A deep understanding of the business aspect of a company is critical. This encompasses areas such as understanding the market, competition, business models, financials, and the key metrics the company cares about. Having a deep understanding of these aspects will enable you to make better decisions about the product and its roadmap.

14. Have a Mentor, Be a Mentor

Seek a mentor in your AI/ML PM journey – someone who's been in your shoes and can provide guidance. Similarly, be open to mentoring others. Mentorship can provide unique perspectives, aid professional development, and bolster networking.

15. Build a Personal Brand

Having a strong personal brand can open doors for opportunities within and outside your organisation. You can build your brand by sharing your insights, learnings, and thoughts on AI/ML trends and technologies. This could be through articles, podcasts, webinars, or even social media platforms.

16. Building Resilience

Resilience is the ability to adapt and bounce back when things don't go as planned. As an AI/ML PM, you'll likely face numerous setbacks - failed product launches, missed targets, and difficult stakeholders, among others. Resilience will enable you to learn from these experiences and come back stronger.

17. Network, Network, Network

Building and nurturing professional relationships within your field can offer tremendous benefits. From gaining new insights to identifying job opportunities, networking plays a crucial role in career advancement. Attend industry events, join online communities, and don't underestimate the power of a coffee chat.

18. Cultivate a Growth Mindset

Adopting a growth mindset – the belief that you can develop your abilities and intelligence through dedication and hard work – can drive your performance and professional growth. It will encourage you to embrace challenges, persist in the face of setbacks, see effort as the path to mastery, learn from criticism, and find lessons and inspiration in the success of others.

In conclusion, succeeding and advancing in your AI/ML Product Manager career requires a multifaceted approach. There is no one-size-fits-all strategy, but the aspects outlined above provide a roadmap to guide your journey. By prioritising learning, developing essential skills, and staying agile in the face of technological advancements, you can navigate the dynamic AI/ML landscape with confidence and success. Always remember the AI/ML PM journey is a marathon, not a sprint.

Chapter 19

Building Relationships
and Influence

As an AI and ML Product Manager, your remit extends beyond the technical and strategic management of your product. It involves orchestrating various stakeholders, managing expectations, and aligning different viewpoints towards a shared goal. Essential to these tasks is your ability to build relationships and wield influence effectively.

Developing Strong Relationships

The essence of cultivating strong relationships lies in grasping the needs, motivations, and concerns of your counterparts. In the world of AI and ML product management, these counterparts could be engineers, data scientists, UX designers, marketing teams, or C-suite executives. Each role brings unique perspectives and challenges to the table.

The first step towards building strong relationships is to arrange regular meetings with these stakeholders. This encourages open dialogue and facilitates a better understanding of each other's roles and objectives. These conversations serve as a platform to share ideas, concerns, and visions for the product, creating a symbiotic relationship of shared knowledge and mutual growth.

By actively listening during these exchanges, you do more than just make the other party feel valued and heard. You immerse yourself in their world, gaining a broader view of your product's impact across the business and the market. This understanding not only allows you to take informed decisions but also enables you to become a better advocate for your product, both internally and externally.

As you forge these relationships, remember the power of empathy. The ability to step into the shoes of your colleagues and appreciate their challenges deepens your connection. It breeds mutual respect, fostering an environment where everyone feels comfortable sharing their ideas and concerns, leading to more robust and innovative product outcomes.

Another cornerstone of relationship-building is demonstrating reliability.

Reliability extends beyond merely keeping your promises. It encompasses being there for your stakeholders in times of challenge and uncertainty. Whether it's aiding your engineering team in resolving a technical impasse or supporting your marketing team in crafting the perfect product narrative, your support underscores your commitment to shared success.

Maintaining transparency in your communications is also crucial. Honest and clear communication reduces the scope for misunderstanding and nurtures trust. By ensuring stakeholders are regularly updated about product developments, strategy shifts, or even potential setbacks, you establish yourself as a trustworthy and reliable leader. This trust forms the bedrock of strong, sustainable relationships.

In essence, strong relationships are not about transactional interactions but about fostering a shared understanding, mutual respect, and a common vision. By understanding the needs and challenges of your stakeholders, providing unwavering support, and upholding transparency, you can create lasting alliances. These relationships will not only make your role as an AI and ML Product Manager more rewarding but also contribute significantly to the success and efficacy of your product management strategies.

Exerting Influence

Influence, in the realm of product management, is not about exerting dominance or pressuring others to accept your viewpoint. Rather, it's about persuasively communicating the merit of your ideas and fostering an environment that encourages consensus and collaboration. It's about inspiring trust, respect, and commitment from your team and stakeholders, and the path to this begins with establishing your credibility as a leader.

Leadership credibility stems from your knowledge, your ability to make sound decisions, and, importantly, the way you interact with your team and stakeholders. In the AI and ML landscape, it's crucial to continually update your technical knowledge and stay abreast of the latest trends and advancements. This not only enables you to make informed decisions but also sends a powerful message to your team about your commitment and competence.

When it comes to decision-making, adopt an approach that blends data-driven analysis with empathy. While it's crucial to base decisions on hard facts and data, especially in AI and ML domains, considering the human element strengthens your leadership. Acknowledge the efforts of your team, appreciate their skills, and consider their viewpoints. This balanced approach enhances your credibility and naturally increases your influence.

The quality of your relationships also significantly impacts your ability to influence. Strong relationships built on mutual trust and respect form a fertile ground for influence to thrive. When you understand and value your stakeholders' perspectives, they are more likely to be receptive to your ideas.

Remember, wielding influence is also about your communication skills. Present your ideas clearly and convincingly, providing logical arguments backed by data. But beyond presenting, learn to listen, too. Incorporate feedback and demonstrate flexibility where needed. This not only enriches your ideas but also underscores your collaborative spirit.

Influencing others, then, is a delicate art that balances your competence as a leader with your ability to foster strong, respectful relationships. It's a continual process, evolving with each interaction, each decision, and each challenge. But when done right, it can be a powerful tool, driving your team towards shared goals, aligning diverse perspectives, and ultimately steering your AI and ML products towards success.

Speak the language of your audience. When discussing technical matters with engineers or data scientists, ensure you grasp the concepts well enough to converse convincingly. When dealing with executives, present your ideas in a business context, highlighting potential impact on revenue, cost savings, or competitive advantage. By tailoring your communication style, you increase the likelihood of your message resonating with your audience.

Foster a culture of collaboration. Frame your initiatives as team efforts rather than individual endeavours. Be open to ideas and ensure every member feels heard and appreciated. This inclusivity encourages others to buy into your vision and contribute proactively.

Equally important is your ability to manage conflict. Disagreements are inevitable, but it's your response that determines the outcome. Aim to de-escalate tension, keep discussions fact-based, and strive for solutions that, while may not be perfect, are agreeable to all parties. Showing maturity in handling disagreements enhances your influence and earns you respect.

The ability to build relationships and influence effectively is a cornerstone of a successful AI and ML Product Manager's career. It's a skill set that necessitates patience, empathy, and consistent effort. However, the payoff is substantial, aiding you in driving your vision, managing team dynamics, and facilitating the successful delivery of AI and ML products that truly make a difference.

Remember, the journey of an AI and ML Product Manager is an ongoing one, filled with continuous learning and relationship-building. By honing your interpersonal skills and understanding the art of influence, you'll be better equipped to navigate the dynamic and challenging landscape of AI and ML product management, thereby paving the way for a successful, fulfilling career.

Chapter 20

Staying Up to Date

in AI/ML

The dynamic and ever-evolving landscape of artificial intelligence and machine learning requires AI and ML Product Managers to be on a constant journey of learning and discovery. To be effective in this role, you must stay abreast of the latest advancements, trends, and challenges. This chapter aims to guide you through the various methods of keeping your knowledge up-to-date in the fast-paced world of AI and ML.

Subscribing to Leading Industry Publications

An excellent starting point is to familiarise yourself with industry-specific publications. Leading journals, newsletters, blogs, and podcasts in the AI and ML fields offer insights into new developments, breakthroughs, and emerging trends. Some highly recommended resources include 'The AI Alignment Podcast', 'MIT Technology Review', 'ArXiv', and 'Towards Data Science'. By dedicating time each day to these resources, you can stay well-informed and gain perspectives from thought leaders and pioneers in the field.

Attending Webinars, Workshops, and Conferences

Webinars, workshops, and conferences are valuable platforms for learning from experts and networking with fellow professionals. Events such as 'NeurIPS', 'ICML', and 'O'Reilly AI Conference present opportunities to explore the latest research, tools, and techniques. Interacting with researchers, data scientists, and other AI and ML Product Managers at these events can broaden your understanding and expose you to new ideas.

Engaging in Continuous Learning

Continuous learning is essential for an AI and ML Product Manager. Online platforms like Coursera, edX, and Udacity provide a plethora of courses in AI and ML. Attending these courses can deepen your understanding of complex topics and keep you updated on new techniques and tools. Additionally, consider earning relevant certifications, as these can validate your knowledge and competence.

Participating in Online Communities

Online communities such as GitHub, Stack Overflow, and various AI and ML forums are treasure troves of real-world challenges and solutions. Engaging in these communities allows you to learn from the collective experiences of professionals worldwide. Additionally, participating in these forums helps you keep abreast of common challenges and innovative solutions, providing a practical complement to your theoretical knowledge.

Applying Knowledge Through Hands-On Work

Finally, remember that there's no substitute for hands-on experience. Applying the latest techniques and tools in your work can cement your learning and provide insights that reading alone cannot offer. Take on projects that challenge you, collaborate with your data science team, and seize opportunities to experiment with new tools and technologies.

Following Thought Leaders on Social Media

Many AI and ML experts and influencers share their insights on social media platforms like LinkedIn, Twitter, and Medium. Following these thought leaders can keep you informed about the latest trends and debates in the field. Engaging in these discussions can also sharpen your understanding and expose you to diverse viewpoints.

Embracing a Growth Mindset

The rapid pace of advancement in AI and ML demands a growth mindset. Embrace change, remain curious, and don't be afraid to venture into unfamiliar territories. Remember, every new algorithm, tool, or technique you learn adds to your repertoire and makes you a more effective AI and ML Product Manager.

In conclusion, staying up-to-date in AI and ML is a multifaceted process. It involves reading widely, networking, continuous learning, active participation in online communities, hands-on application, social media engagement, and above all, a growth mindset. By adopting these practices, you can navigate the exciting and challenging landscape of AI and ML product management with confidence and competence, thereby boosting your career prospects and contributing more effectively to your organisation's AI and ML endeavours.

Chapter 21

Career Advancement

for AI/ML PMs

Embarking on a journey as an AI and ML Product Manager (PM) can be
both challenging and exhilarating. The key to flourishing in this realm lies in honing your skills, acquiring knowledge, building relationships, and focusing on your career trajectory. This chapter will provide you with a roadmap to navigate your path and advance your career in AI and ML product management.

Building a Robust Skillset

The success of an AI and ML PM pivots on a balanced amalgamation of technical knowledge, strategic thinking, and people skills. Alongside a robust understanding of AI and ML concepts, it is vital to develop strong business acumen. Understanding business metrics, market trends, and user behaviour helps you steer your product towards success. Furthermore, improving soft skills, such as leadership, communication, and empathy, aids in managing teams and fostering productive relationships.

Embracing Continuous Learning

Staying ahead in the fast-paced world of AI and ML requires continuous learning. Keep yourself abreast of the latest developments, algorithms, tools, and techniques. Be it through online courses, webinars, or conferences, immerse yourself in learning. Certifications in relevant areas can enhance your credibility, equipping you with the skills to tackle complex product challenges.

Creating a Track Record of Success

Creating a successful portfolio of products is a powerful way to demonstrate your capabilities as an AI and ML Product Manager. This involves not only the successful launch of new products but also the careful cultivation of each product's lifecycle, ensuring their continuing relevance and impact. However, achieving this isn't just about ticking off a checklist of product features or meeting deadlines. It's about showcasing your aptitude in addressing real-world problems, delivering value to your organisation and its customers, and driving consistent, meaningful results.

In the context of AI and ML, a successful product could be an intelligent system that improves operational efficiency, a predictive model that enhances decision-making, or an ML-driven application that elevates user experience. The impact of your product is gauged by how effectively it addresses a need, how substantially it contributes to business objectives, and how well it keeps up with (or, better yet, anticipates) market trends.

Being able to demonstrate this success requires more than just narrating your achievements. It's about articulating the problem your product solved, the strategy you adopted, the challenges you overcame, and the results you delivered. These success narratives, coupled with quantifiable results—improved customer satisfaction, increased revenue, or reduced operational costs—add credibility to your track record.

Remember that success in product management isn't solely about the end product. It's also about the journey. Showcasing your ability to lead cross-functional teams, handle complex trade-offs, manage stakeholder expectations, and navigate the uncertain waters of AI and ML development can strengthen your reputation as a competent and reliable PM.

Furthermore, success should be viewed through the lens of learning and growth. Even products that didn't meet initial expectations can contribute to your track record. They provide opportunities to demonstrate your ability to learn from experience, adapt your strategies, and show resilience in the face of challenges. These are qualities that organisations value immensely, particularly in the dynamic world of AI and ML.

Develop a habit of documenting your successes, big and small. Maintain a detailed record of the projects you've handled, the solutions you've delivered, and the impact you've created. This will serve as your personal catalogue of achievements and learnings, a valuable resource when seeking career advancements or presenting your capabilities to stakeholders.

Networking and Building Influence

The strength of your relationships within the industry and your organisation can significantly impact your career growth. Attend industry events and workshops, participate in online communities, and engage with other product professionals. Build a reputation as a reliable and competent product leader, someone who can bring people together and drive a shared vision.

Seeking Mentorship

Identify seasoned professionals who inspire you and seek their mentorship. Mentors can provide valuable guidance, broaden your perspective, and offer insights gained from their years of experience. Regular interactions with your mentors can boost your confidence and provide you with a sounding board for your ideas and strategies.

Planning for the Next Steps

As you mature in your role, take the time to reflect on your career path. Do you aspire to move into a senior product leadership role, or are you more inclined towards a specialised path, like focusing on a specific AI/ML domain? Charting your path and setting clear career goals will enable you to focus your efforts and navigate your career progression effectively.

Adopting a Leadership Role

As your experience grows, so does your responsibility to guide others. Mentoring junior product managers and leading initiatives not only boosts your team's overall competence but also strengthens your leadership skills. Being seen as a thought leader who can inspire and educate others can propel your career advancement.

In conclusion, advancing your career as an AI and ML PM is a multifaceted journey. It involves augmenting your skills, continuously updating your knowledge, demonstrating success, fostering relationships, seeking mentorship, planning your career path, and adopting a leadership role. The path may seem daunting, but remember, each step you take builds on the last, shaping you into a successful and influential AI and ML Product Manager. Keep learning, stay resilient, and be ready to embrace the opportunities and challenges that come your way as you chart your course in the exciting world of AI and ML product management.

Chapter 22

Continuous

Learning and Growth

Embarking on a career in AI and ML Product Management means committing oneself to a path of relentless growth and learning. The speed and magnitude at which the AI and ML fields evolve demand a constant focus on expanding your knowledge base, sharpening your skills, and staying attuned to the latest trends and developments.

Continuous Learning: A Prerequisite

The ethos of continuous learning is more than a professional obligation; it is a driving force that propels you to new heights. It not only keeps you relevant in an ever-evolving industry but also ensures your product decisions are informed, timely, and impactful. With AI and ML at the heart of your role, it's imperative to keep up with the advances in algorithms, software tools, computing technology, data handling, and ethical guidelines.

Such an endeavour can be facilitated through numerous avenues. Online courses, webinars, and certifications offer structured learning pathways, often culminating in a tangible testament to your advanced skills. Meanwhile, reputable journals, research publications, industry reports, and thought-leader blogs provide in-depth insights into the latest breakthroughs and trends in the AI and ML space.

There's much to be gained from participation in industry conferences and networking events. Apart from knowledge acquisition, these platforms offer opportunities to connect with peers, share ideas, and gain exposure to diverse perspectives. A diverse professional network can prove invaluable, fostering idea exchange and collaboration and, often, paving the way for career advancement.

323

The Art of Growing through Challenges

Learning in the field of AI and ML product management isn't confined to formal education or informational resources. In fact, some of the most profound learning experiences arise from confronting and overcoming real-world challenges.

Navigating complex product trade-offs, aligning disparate stakeholder views, managing resource constraints, or addressing ethical dilemmas in AI usage – these are all opportunities for growth. Each challenge overcome not only deepens your expertise but also sharpens your problem-solving abilities, resilience, and leadership skills.

It's equally important to embrace failures as learning experiences. Each setback encountered in your product management journey provides invaluable lessons. Whether it's a product feature that didn't resonate with users, a flawed go-to-market strategy, or an overlooked AI bias, each misstep can be transformed into a stepping stone towards improvement.

Promoting a Learning Culture

As a product manager, your commitment to learning and growth extends beyond personal development. You are uniquely positioned to foster a culture of learning within your team and the broader organisation. Encourage your team to stay updated with the latest AI and ML trends, facilitate knowledge-sharing sessions, and provide the necessary support for their skill development.

Promoting a learning culture also involves cultivating an environment that encourages experimentation and tolerates failures. Innovations in AI and ML often require venturing into the unknown, taking calculated risks, and learning from the outcomes. By fostering such a culture, you are not only enhancing the collective competencies of your team but also nurturing an environment conducive to innovation and growth.

Embracing the Future

As you chart your course in the dynamic world of AI and ML Product Management, remember that continuous learning and growth aren't merely strategies for career progression. They're the lifeblood that fuels your ability to make impactful decisions, lead with confidence, and, ultimately, shape the future of AI and ML in your organisation.

The role of an AI and ML Product Manager is demanding yet rewarding, fraught with challenges yet brimming with opportunities. By embracing continuous learning, adapting to change, and turning setbacks into learning, you can navigate this complex landscape with agility and poise.

In doing so, you are not only securing your professional relevance but also contributing meaningfully to the exciting, transformative realm of AI and ML.

Reflections

Embarking on the journey of an AI and ML Product Manager, one is stepping into a domain that sits at the confluence of technology, strategy, and human impact. It's a realm teeming with innovation and possibilities, with challenges as intense as the opportunities it presents.

Reflecting upon this journey, it's pertinent to recognise that the essence of an AI and ML Product Manager role transcends the sphere of technology. At its heart, it's about leveraging AI and ML's transformative capabilities to create products that truly matter. It's about building solutions that solve real-world problems, that make people's lives better, and that fuel progress in myriad sectors of society.

This role isn't without its share of challenges. From grappling with the technical intricacies of AI and ML, navigating the evolving landscape of data privacy and ethics, to managing diverse stakeholders and driving alignment - it's a role that demands a versatile skill set. But with each challenge surmounted, there's a profound sense of accomplishment and growth, a testament to your resilience, ingenuity, and leadership.

Our journey through this playbook, from understanding the fundamentals of AI and ML to exploring the nuances of product management, interview preparations, and career advancement strategies, is akin to navigating the trajectory of an AI and ML Product Manager. It's a journey marked by continuous learning, relentless pursuit of excellence, and a commitment to making a meaningful impact.

As you stand at this junction, ready to steer your career in the AI and ML product management direction, you carry with you not just the technical and strategic knowledge but also the ethos that underpins a successful career in this domain. The ethos of empathetic leadership, of building relationships and wielding influence, of staying attuned to the pulse of AI and ML advancements, and of embracing continuous learning and growth.

Each step taken in this journey, every challenge confronted, and every success celebrated is a brick in the edifice of your career as an AI and ML Product Manager. As you step forward, remember that the power of AI and ML is as much about the transformative products you create as it is about the journey of growth, discovery, and impact you embark upon.

Reflecting upon the landscape of AI and ML Product Management, one can't help but feel a sense of awe at the transformative power of this domain. It's a domain that's shaping the future of how we live, work, and interact, with AI and ML Product Managers at the helm, steering this transformative wave.

As you close this chapter of your journey and embark on the next, bear in mind that your role as an AI and ML Product Manager is not just a job. It's a mission – a mission to leverage AI and ML to create products that matter, to solve problems that count, and to shape the future in ways that make a difference.

In the world of AI and ML Product Management, you're not just a technologist or a strategist; you're a change-maker, an innovator, and a leader. And as you venture forth in your journey, remember that every step you take is a step towards making a meaningful impact in the exciting, transformative realm of AI and ML.

Here's to your journey, to the challenges you'll conquer, the successes you'll celebrate, the lives you'll impact, and the future you'll shape. Here's to the journey of an AI and ML Product Manager - a journey of endless learning, relentless innovation, and profound impact. Here's to you.

Next Steps

As you reach the final pages of 'From Zero to Offer: The AI & ML Product Manager's Interview Playbook', you find yourself standing at the threshold of an exciting journey, equipped with a wealth of knowledge and insights. But the learning doesn't end here; rather, it's the start of your continuing education in the ever-evolving landscape of AI and ML product management.

The first step forward is to consolidate what you've learnt. Reflect on each chapter, the concepts, strategies, and skills you've acquired. Understand how each element interweaves to create the fabric of an AI and ML Product Manager's role.

Next, create a learning roadmap. Identify the areas where you feel you need more proficiency. It could be a deeper understanding of AI algorithms, enhancing your leadership skills, or getting more hands-on experience with data analysis tools. Once you have identified these areas, devise a plan to further your knowledge. This could involve enrolling in specialised courses, attending webinars, or simply reading more about the subject.

Parallel to this academic endeavour, immerse yourself in the practical world of AI and ML. Engage with AI and ML communities, both online and offline. Participate in discussions, share your insights, and learn from the experiences of others. This not only enriches your understanding but also helps you build a strong professional network.

Embrace the culture of continuous innovation that is intrinsic to AI and ML. Stay attuned to the latest developments, emerging trends, the path-breaking products. Read widely, be it research papers, case studies, or tech blogs. Keep your finger on the pulse of the industry; this will not only keep your knowledge current but also help you identify opportunities and anticipate challenges.

As you chart your career path in AI and ML product management, it's important to gain hands-on experience. Seek internships or projects within your organisation that allow you to apply what you've learned. Practical experience not only solidifies your learning but also provides invaluable insights that can't be acquired from books or courses.

Developing your personal brand is another crucial step. Establish yourself as a thought leader in the field. Write articles or blogs, give talks or webinars, and share your insights on professional platforms. A strong personal brand can open doors to opportunities and play a pivotal role in career advancement.

As you tread the path of career advancement, don't lose sight of the value of mentorship. Seek guidance from those who have traversed the path before you. Their experiences, their insights, and their advice can provide valuable navigation aids for your journey.

Lastly, but most importantly, cultivate resilience and adaptability. The world of AI and ML is characterised by rapid, often unpredictable changes. Embrace these changes, learn from them, adapt, and grow. Resilience and adaptability are the compass and anchor that will guide and steady you through the ebbs and flows of this dynamic landscape.

Remember, your journey as an AI and ML Product Manager is more than a career path; it's a voyage of constant discovery, of pushing boundaries and creating impact. The following steps you take are towards shaping the future, solving real-world problems, and towards making a difference through the power of AI and ML.

With this, we close our journey through this playbook, but your journey continues. The final message, and perhaps the most important one, is this - always keep learning, keep growing, keep innovating, and keep making a difference. The world of AI and ML product management awaits you, teeming with opportunities and challenges, ready to be shaped by your ideas and efforts.

NOTES

1. **Preface:** A snapshot of the book's content, outlining the journey from understanding AI/ML to succeeding as an AI/ML Product Manager.
2. **Welcome:** This section sets the stage, giving readers an introduction to the scope and relevance of the book.
3. **Objectives of the Book:** The book aims to provide comprehensive insights into AI/ML product management, equipping readers with the knowledge, skills, and strategies to excel in AI/ML product management roles.
4. **How to Use This Book:** A guide on navigating the book effectively, highlighting how each part builds on the previous to deliver a holistic understanding of AI/ML product management.
5. **Part I: Foundation of AI/ML Product Management:**
   - **Chapter 1: Understanding AI/ML:** An overview of AI/ML, exploring key concepts and technologies.
   - **Chapter 2: Role of a Product Manager in AI/ML:** An in-depth look at the Responsibilities and challenges of an AI/ML Product Manager.
   - **Chapter 3: Essential Skills for AI/ML Product Managers:** Outlines the unique blend of skills necessary for AI/ML Product Managers, including technical acumen, leadership, and strategic thinking.

6. **Part II: Preparing for Your AI/ML PM Interview:**
   - **Chapter 4: Understanding the AI/ML PM Job Market:** Offers a detailed analysis of the current job market, including trends and opportunities in the AI/ML product management sphere.
   - **Chapter 5: Crafting an Impactful AI/ML PM Resume:** Provides tips for creating a powerful resume that highlights relevant experiences and skills.
   - **Chapter 6: Writing a Convincing Cover Letter:** Discuss strategies to write a compelling cover letter tailored to AI/ML product management roles.
   - **Chapter 7: Conducting In-depth Company Research:** Highlights the importance of company research before an interview and offers effective methods for gathering valuable information.
   - **Chapter 8: Effective Networking Strategies:** Outlines how networking can open doors to opportunities and provides strategies for effective networking.
   - **Chapter 9: Decoding the Job Description:** Guides readers on how to dissect a job description to understand the expectations and requirements of the role better.
7. **Part III: The AI/ML PM Interview Process:**
   - **Chapter 10: The Screening Interview:** Offers insights into the initial screening phase, including potential questions and how to prepare.

- Chapter 11: The Technical Interview: Discusses the technical aspects of AI/ML product management interviews and offers tips to navigate them effectively.
- Chapter 12: The Behavioral Interview: Examines the importance of soft skills in product management and offers strategies to showcase these during interviews.
- Chapter 13: The Case Study Interview: Highlights the crucial role case studies play in AI/ML PM interviews, with strategies for effective preparation and presentation.
- Chapter 14: The On-site Interview: Provides insights into the final phase of the interview process, including expectations and tips for success.
- Chapter 15: Negotiating Your Offer: Explores strategies for effective negotiation, ensuring the best possible job offer.

8. Part IV: Interviewing Mastery:
   - Chapter 16: Common AI/ML PM Interview Questions: Lists common interview questions for AI/ML PM roles, providing strategies for effective responses.
   - Chapter 17: Post-Interview Tips: Offers guidance on steps to take after the interview, including follow-ups and reflections.

9. Part V: Succeeding and Advancing in Your AI/ML Product Manager Career:
   - Chapter 18: The First 90 Days: Outlines strategies to make the most of the critical initial period in a new role.

- ○ **Chapter 19: Building Relationships and Influence:** Discusses the importance of building strong relationships and influence within the organisation.
- ○ **Chapter 20: Staying Up to Date in AI/ML:** Highlights the necessity of continuous learning in the rapidly evolving AI/ML field.
- ○ **Chapter 21: Career Advancement for AI/ML PMs:** Provides guidance on career progression in AI/ML product management.
- ○ **Chapter 22: Continuous Learning and Growth:** Emphasises the importance of a culture of continuous learning and growth.

10. **Conclusion:** Final thoughts on the journey of becoming an AI/ML Product Manager and the importance of continual growth.
11. **Reflections:** A reflective chapter to assess learning and growth.
12. **Next Steps:** Guides readers on how to put their learning into practice, with an emphasis on lifelong learning.
13. **Appendices:** Additional resources and materials to support the reader's learning journey.
14. **Notes:** An overview of important points from each chapter, serving as a quick reference guide.
15. **Bibliography:** Cites the sources of information used throughout the book.
16. **About the Author:** Provides a brief bio of the author, their credentials, and their motivation for writing the book.

BIBLIOGRAPHY

1. SiteGarden. (2023, April 16). "Understanding Machine Learning from the Ground Up." Retrieved from www.sitegarden.nukebox.com.
2. DesignGurus. (2023, March 10). "The Role of AI in Product Design." Retrieved from www.designgurus.io.
3. SmashWords. (2023, February 2). "AI and Machine Learning: A New Paradigm for Product Management." Retrieved from www.smashwords.com.
4. Scribd. (2023, May 12). "Strategies for Landing a Product Manager Job in the AI Industry." Retrieved from es.scribd.com.
5. CourseHero. (2023, January 15). "Case Study: AI & ML Product Management." Retrieved from www.coursehero.com.
6. EvolvedEnterprise. (2023, April 30). "AI in Business: An Enterprise Perspective." Retrieved from evolvedenterprise.com.
7. UrduNama. (2022, December 20). "International Perspectives on AI and ML Product Management." Retrieved from urdunama.org.
8. RedBlink. (2022, November 11). "The Future of AI and ML in Product Management." Retrieved from redblink.com.
9. DASLS. (2023, March 3). "Legal Considerations in AI and ML Products." Retrieved from www.dasls.com.
10. ResearchGate. (2023, January 20). "Scholarly Research on AI and ML Product Management." Retrieved from www.researchgate.net.
11. Exeter University. (2022, September 30). "AI and ML in Higher Education: A Case Study." Retrieved from ore.exeter.ac.uk.
12. Madera Tribune. (2023, April 1). "How AI and ML are Transforming Local Businesses." Retrieved from www.maderatribune.com.
13. IJIRCCE. (2023, February 5). "The Impact of AI and ML on Communication Engineering." Retrieved from ijircce.com.

14. BusinessManiac. (2022, December 12). "AI & ML: A Business Perspective." Retrieved from businessmaniac.beepworld.de.
15. VNExplorer. (2023, May 30). "AI and ML Developments in Vietnam." Retrieved from vnexplorer.net.
16. DesignFitLife. (2023, March 25). "The Intersection of Design, Fitness and AI." Retrieved from designfitlife.com.
17. Forbes. (2023, February 18). "AI and ML: The Next Big Thing in Product Management." Retrieved from www.forbes.com.
18. Medium. (2022, October 15). "The Role of AI and ML in the Modern Digital Landscape." Retrieved from medium.com.
19. The Glass Hammer. (2023, June 5). "Women in AI and ML Product Management." Retrieved from theglasshammer.com.

About the author

Luis Jurado is an accomplished Product Manager Coach with more than a decade of experience in Product Management and Product Manager Coaching. He is highly regarded as an industry thought leader, widely known for his strategic innovation and ability to bring together a team with diverse perspectives. Luis is an author of the book "The AI-Powered Product Manager: Combining Strategy and Technology," which showcases his profound knowledge in both technology and strategy, with an emphasis on AI-driven products.

Throughout his illustrious career, Luis has been celebrated for his prowess in coaching product managers and developing transformative product strategies. His passion for imparting knowledge and creating products that prioritize users' needs has significantly influenced many professionals to grow and thrive in their respective careers.

Luis's unique success recipe lies in fostering a collaborative, team-oriented culture. His interpersonal skills make him adept at managing both internal and external stakeholders, ensuring fluid communication and efficient work processes. His in-depth market knowledge, combined with a keen sense for identifying trends and opportunities, enables him to consistently devise and implement innovative strategies that steer his products towards success.

Away from the hustle and bustle of his professional life, Luis is an avid conversationalist who thrives on meeting new people and engaging in intellectually stimulating conversations over a cup of coffee. This genuine interest in others and a commitment to his own continuous learning and personal growth ensures he stays on the cutting edge of the ever-evolving landscape of machine learning and AI-powered Product Management.

In a nutshell, Luis Jurado is an industry pioneer and a visionary leader, dedicated to revolutionizing Product Management with a keen eye on AI-driven technologies. His passion for creating user-centric products and his unique approach to leadership have paved the way for others in the field, further cementing his reputation as an influential figure in the Product Manager Coaching sphere. His book is a testament to his extensive experience and in-depth knowledge, a valuable guide for anyone aspiring to succeed in the rapidly advancing world of AI and product management.

L U I S   J U R A D O

Web: https://www.luisjurado.me/
LinkedIn @mrluisjurado

representation or warranties with respect to the accuracy or completeness of the contents of this book and specifically disclaim any implied warranties of merchantability or fitness for a particular purpose and shall in no event be liable for any loss of profit or any other commercial damage, including but not limited to special, incidental, consequential, or other damages.

Any trademarks, service marks, product names, or named features are assumed to be the property of their respective owners and are used only for reference. There is no implied endorsement if one of these terms is used.

The author acknowledges the trademarked status and trademark owners of various products referenced in this work, which have been used without permission. The publication/use of these trademarks is not authorised, associated with, or sponsored by the trademark owners.
For more information about the author and their other works, please visit https://www.luisjurado.me/.

Printed in Great Britain
by Amazon

43031321R00188